WEB TECHNOLOGIES IN LIBRARY AND INFORMATION SCIENCE

WEB TECHNOLOGIES IN LIBRARY AND INFORMATION SCIENCE

Dr. P. BALASUBRAMANIAN
M.A., M.L.I.Sc., M.Phil., PGDCA, PGDPR, Ph.D.
Deputy Librarian
Manonmaniam Sundaranar University
Tirunelveli (T.N.)

REGAL PUBLICATIONS
New Delhi - 110 027

WEB TECHNOLOGIES IN LIBRARY
AND INFORMATION SCIENCE

ISBN 978-81-8484-164-0

Typeset by
RAHUL COMPOSERS
358, Pocket-B, Phase-2, Sector-16 B, Dwarka, New Delhi - 110 075

Printed in India at
MAYUR ENTERPRISES
WZ Plot No. 3, Gujjar Market, Tihar Village, New Delhi - 110 018

Published by
REGAL PUBLICATIONS
F-159, Rajouri Garden, New Delhi - 110 027 • Phone : 45546396
E-mail : regalbookspub@yahoo.com

Contents

PART II
WEB RESOURCES

PART III

BROWSERS AND SEARCH ENGINES

PART IV
WEB TECHNOLOGY

PART V
DIGITAL LIBRARY

Acknowledgements

The author feels extremely indebted to Dr. K.A. Manikumar, Director (DD & CE) Manonmaniam Sundaranar University, Tirunelveli and all the teaching and Non-teaching staff members of the M.S. University for giving me constant encouragement for writing this Book.

I also thank Prof. Dr. A. Rangaswamy, Professor, Management Studies, Infant Jesus College of Engineering, Thoothukudi for help and suggestions.

I would like to thank my beloved wife Mrs. B. Devi and my sweet children who shared my burden and helped me many ways during the preparation of this book.

My thanks are due to Mr. A. Ravisankar, for computerising the manuscript so nicely.

I would be a benefit killer if I do not acknowledge the services of Regal Publications, New Delhi for their efforts in bringing out this book in a record time.

Suggestions for further improvement of the books are most welcome.

DR. P. BALASUBRAMANIAN

Acknowledgements

PART I

Internet Technology

1

Basics of Internet

1. HOW DID THE INTERNET DEVELOP?

In the 1960s, the Advanced Research Project Agency (ARPA) of United States funded a research project. The project was to connect computer engineers and scientists working in Universities by means of computers. The physical layer included use of the telephone line, and what is now called POTS: Plain Old Telephone System. This project was called ARPANET. Soon ARPANET became extremely useful for the university researchers.

A protocol is a program that executes tasks in a network in a standardized manner. It has a standard set of headers for transfer requests, environmental variables, fields, parameters, methods, status code definitions, and negotiation methods between a sender and receiver or a client and a server. [Refer to http://www.sei.cmu.edu/str/descriptions/clientserver.html for a detailed description of the client-server architecture in detail]. ARPANET users started sharing the resources of the computers by tele-networking using a protocol called Telnet. This protocol shares a remote computer's resources through a telephone. File transferring, tele-networking, mailing (called e-mail) were then the main uses. Since researchers in universities mainly used UNIX-based computers (machines) up to late 1970s, ARPANET mainly interconnected the UNIX machines.

In 1975, Vinton Cerf of Stanford University developed a transport layer protocol and reported it in a paper, "A protocol for Packet Network Interconnection" presented at IEEE Transactions on Communication, COM-22, 637-648, May 1974. This protocol is called Transmission Control Protocol (TCP). He also developed a network layer protocol called Internet Protocol (IP). TCP/IP means the use of TCP (or UDP) at the transport layer, and the use of IP at the network layer. The TCP/IP suite of protocols soon became the main standard for computer networking. Meanwhile, Robert Metcalfe developed the Ethernet LAN. The Ethernet LAN soon became the method and main standard at the local level in an organization. The TCP/IP therefore networked these LANs also at the WAN level.

In 1980s, the National Science Foundation (NSF) funded the TCP/IP network to establish a network, NSFNET; Initially NSFNET used digital exchanges and a speed of 56 kbps over the telephone lines. In 1988, it started using the Tl (1.544 Mbps) carrier to network regional networks. These regional networks then hierarchically networked universities in USA. [Note: One kbps means a thousand bits per second and 1 Mbps means a Million bits per second. One character takes eight bits. One line of text takes ~ 750 bits. One page of text is ~ 25000 bits. One Mbps then means ~ 40 pages of text per second.] These regional networks not only networked the host UNIX machines and computer systems at the universities, but also the DOS-based machines, the Ethernet LANs, and personal stand-alone computers. A regional network service provider came into being, analogous to the current-day service provider, Internet Service Provider (ISP). [An ISP is a service provider who connects the user computers, LANs, etc. to the Internet]. A large network of networks following the uniform protocol TCP/IP. took shape through these regional networks and it evolved into what is now a grand the Internet.

From 1988 to 1993, the number of packets communicated grew month. [1 Packet = 2^{16} bytes maximum]. In USA, the main uses base follows:

(i) File transfer.
(ii) E-mail.
(iii) Electronic Bulletin Board.
(iv) Telnet (remote computer share through telephone).
(v) News.
(vi) Chat.

These applications, also called services, are described in Sections 2.4 In 1993, NSFNET networks started using the T3 (45 Mbps) carrier to network a large number and variety of users (hosts). In 1995, the NSF support ended and non-governmental ISPs in the USA took over regional networks. After 1995, NSF support continued only for high-speed optical fiber-based OC-3c (155.52 Mbps) research networks in the universities. NSF-supported services were analogous to the service being provided by current-day **Backbone Service Providers** (BSPs) and **Network Access Point** (NAPs) operators. Using Dense Wavelength Division Multiplexing (DWDM) it is now feasible to obtain 20 Gbps and 40 Gbps rates of data transfer between NAPs.

The next phase of development, Internet II, uses STM-4/ OC12 (622.08 Mbps). It provides very high-speed backbone-network service (vBNS). It forms what is called the Broadband Internet. It provides fast access for streaming video.

2. HOW DID THE WORLD WIDE WEB DEVELOP?

Scientists collaborating in research at the Center for European Research on Nuclear High Energy Particles (CERN) established a computer network like ARPANET for remote collaboration, and for sharing computer resources. In 1992, Tim Berners-Lee, a Swiss software engineer, developed a graphic user interface (GUI)-based tool. He presented a paper entitled "The World Wide Web" at proceedings of the 3rd Joint European Networking Conference, Innsbruck, Austria, in May 1992. The tool was for navigating (searching, sharing, and searching and copying), transfer, and to access documents stored at many computers at CERN. This tool, using the hypertext, became a basis for the **World Wide Web** (also abbreviated as WWW or Web or W3 or w3 or 3w). What is a hypertext? The Web is like an on-line library at our fingertips, providing us constantly updated information relating to a large number of subjects, universities, organizations, companies, and individuals. The Web is at present the global information communication and exchange tool. It is giving a great dimension to the Internet.

A **website** is a document in hypertext form. It possesses texts, files, databases, voice-clips, video-clips, etc. It is used as an access point for other sites in the Internet. Sites are identified by three characters '**www**', placed at the beginning of their names. The Web has now over one million web sites and over 1.4 billion pages. Currently, about 70% of all websites are '**.corns**' (pronounced dot com or point com). The words '.com' are placed at the end of the names of www sites, coms are the sites of commercial organizations and business companies. The web address of a company site often reads: www.companyname.com

The last part of the web address therefore indicates the nature of the site. For instance, web addresses may contain any one of the following:

- **edu** which indicates the sites of educational institutions, universities, etc.
- **net** or *.net.country-code-character-*. For example, 'usa.net' or 'vsnl.net.in' or 'sancharnet.in'.

The Web, with its links to billions of pages, has now become main service on the Internet. A web site can now dynamically generate E-commerce (e-COM) applications and mobile phone-based e-commerce (m-COM) are the recent web applications.

A client's communication to and from a web site server uses the Hypertext Transfer Protocol (HTTP). Its new version is HTTP 1.1. Its proposers are R. Fielding, J. Gettys, J. Mogul, H. Frystyk, and T. Berners Lee. It was first introduced in January

1997 and is assigned a standard, RFC 2068. HTTP 1.1 has standard sets for the following:

(i) Headers for transfer requests and server responses.
(ii) Environmental variables, fields, and parameters.
(iii) Methods and negotiation methods between a sender and receiver or a Client and Server.
(iv) Authentication.
(v) Repeated and persistent communication. (From version 1.1 onwards, many client-requests and responses can be handled per connection).
(vi) Encoding.
(vii) Caching.
(viii) Status code definitions.
(ix) Pipelining (from Version 1.1 onwards) of client-requests and server-responses. The client requests for a processed, dynamically generated page from a web server. The server passes that to a JSP, ASP, or Servlet. The latter respond after analyzing and processing the request. The server then sends the web page that sets and stores at the client's end.
(x) Support to cookies from a client to a server, server to a JSP, ASP, or Servlet. The recipient responds after analyzing and processing the request using the Cookie, and by generating new Cookies that set and store at the client's send. server-response headers, response methods and the environmental variables in detail]. HTTP is a connection-oriented, packet-switched network and uses the TCP/IP service, HTTPS is the Hyper Text Transfer Protocol (HTTP) over the Secure Socket Layer. Secure Socket Layer or SSL is explained in Section 3.9.4. SSL replaces the insecure TCP/IP in HTTPS. Transport Layer Security Layer (TLS) is the new version of SSL. It provides data integrity, authentication, privacy, and illegal access prevention.

A portal in English means a large impressive doorway at the entrance of a building. A **portal in the web** means a website that hosts on a huge web server. It has a large knowledge base. Its presentation is artistic. It has a specific theme and aim. It offers the usual services like, site documents server, search facility, e-mail server, and user registration, as well as specific services like, subscription service or commercial service or directory service or brief case service. Brief case service is the allocation of a disk storage space to a registered user at a portal. User can thus place in secure environment his/her documents, programs and data bases. It differs from an ISP in the sense that the portal provides for Internet services to a specific group of persons, for instance, students, job-seekers, doctors, music lovers, young persons, and health conscious persons. An ISP on the other hand is a general service provider. The following are the exemplary portals.

(i) One portal offering services to a specific group is http://www.meditimes.com. It has doctor-specific features. It is hosted by Dr. Reddy Laboratories of India. It gives specific information on many topics of interest to doctors. It also has links to reputed medical journals. It contains a directory of Indian doctors. Doctors' families can also interact through the portal and plan joint activities like holiday trips.

(ii) Another special-interest portal is *http://www.livizi-com.* It is a health portal for the health aspects of life. It is hosted by the Dr. Reddy Laboratories of India. It has sections: 'medical information', 'family health' and 'healthy living'.

(iii) Another special-interest portal is *http://www.indiatimes.com.* It is a news portal. It gives the national news, international news, stock market news, and economic issues related news. It is hosted by the Times of India group. It also provides the services of free e-mail account, searches, and brief case service.

Other important services on the Internet are FTP, a file-transfer-protocol-based service, news, e-mail, and Telnet. Can we talk using Internet in place of a telephone? Yes, Voice-Over-

Internet facilitates this. Voice-Over-Internet Protocol (VOIP) is a protocol that handles the voice packets on the Internet. Voice data bypass fully or partially the PSTN. A VOIP gateway connects a VOIP client with the Internet which, in turn, connects to another VOIP or PSTN client. VOIP takes care of assembling and disassembling the packets and provides the streaming audio.

By the year 2000, Internet users exceeded 10 crore (100 M).

The Internet is now a globally used computer network that has hundreds of millions of users. The World Wide Web holds extensive information about a large number of subjects, universities, organizations, companies, and individuals and provides many services over the Internet.

3. WHY DO WE CONNECT TO THE INTERNET?

We connect to the Internet to send and receive e-mail. We connect to browse through the World Wide Web and to access information from the www sites. We may want to transfer files to and from remote computers using the FTP. We may want to log-in to a remote computer using the Telnet. [A logging-in means to obtain an ability to use the system and its software, data, and other facilities. A UNIX command for it is 'login'.] We may form a user network through Usenet. We may like to chat with members of our group through a service called Internet Relay Chat (IRC).

We may want to use other popular utilities such as Wide Area Information Service (WAIS), Gopher, Internet fax, Internet-based telephone access service, or a multicast networking. May be we want to do business, trade, pay bills, transfer funds and take part in many such commercial activities, now called the electronic commerce (e-commerce) and m-commerce (mobile commerce). New applications are emerging such as video broadcasting by web-casting technology.

The number of Internet users and uses are growing phenomenally. Presently, many services are available through the Internet. The main list is as follows:

(i) E-mail.
(ii) World Wide Web.
(iii) FTP and anonymous FTP.
(iv) Telnet.
(v) News and USENET.
(vi) The Gopher.
(vii) Wide Area Information Service (WAIS).
(viii) Internet Relay Chat (IRC). (be) VOIP.
(ix) WAP.
(x) Web Casting of Video.
(xi) e-COM.
(xii) m-COM.

A computer user connects to the Internet for e-mail, web searching and for many other services. For example, file transfers, Telnet sessions. It is becoming an essential like a telephone.

A transfer means a copy of a file, message, or data-base from one system to another. A session means a period during which an execution, an application, a connection, or a logging-in occurs.

4. HOW DO CONNECTIVITY OCCUR ON THE INTERNET?

Figure 1.1 shows various modes by which an ISP connects to various users and organizations. Figure 1.2 shows how the ISPs interconnect.

Internet Service Providers (ISPs) connect to hosts or individual users and organizations. An ISP host connection to a user may have as low a speed as 28 kbps, when there is a 33.3 kbps modem and a POTS telephone line. Using the Digital Subscriber Line (DSL) to connect to the ISP (for multiple data, voice, and video on a pair of wires) allows two-way conference and data-interchange, operating at 34 kbps and gives 56 kbps speed. Asymmetric DSL (ADSL) gives one way 1.5 to 8 Mbps performance.

Section 1.6.10 referred to the use of GSM and GPRS for the mobile systems for the wireless Internet. GSM and GPRS mobile phones operate at carrier frequencies of 900 MHz and 1800 MHz. [A carrier frequency is a frequency at which the data transmits after modulation that frequency.] Using the GSM, 13-14 kbps Internet data is sent on the mobile wireless communication system that connects to an ISP. Using the GPRS, 115 kbps Internet data connect from the mobile system to the ISP.

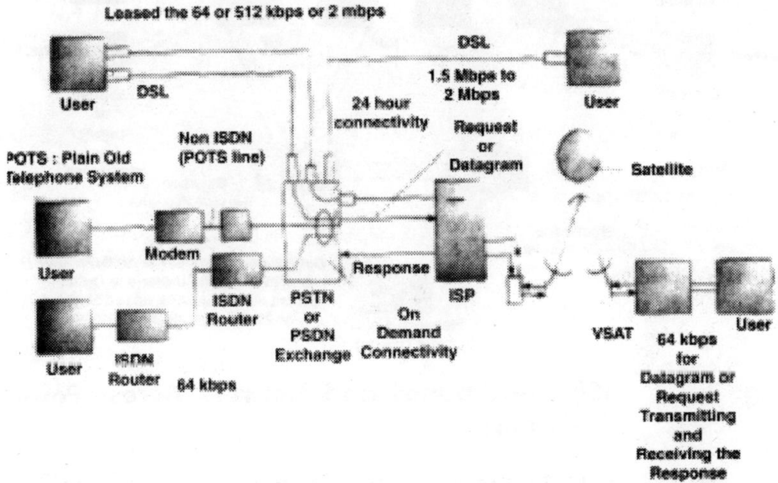

Fig. 1.1 : A user Interconnections through the ISPs (Internet Service Providers).

When there are many hosts (users) in an organization, then there is an ISP-Ethernet LAN or other LAN interconnections made through a leased, dedicated, digital exchange line at 64 kbps. The connection may also be made through an ISDN line using a router. The speed is then either 64 kbps (fractional Tl), 128 kbps (also fractional Tl), or 1.544 Mbps (Full Tl).

Then, there are the Backbone Service Providers that interconnect the ISPs. This interconnection can be :

(i) at medium speed Tl at 1.544 Mbps,
(ii) at high speed T3 at 45 Mbps, or DS-3 also at 45 Mbps, or
(iii) at fast speed through the Synchronous Optical Network (SONET) OC-1 at 55.840 Mbps or OC-3C at 155 Mbps.

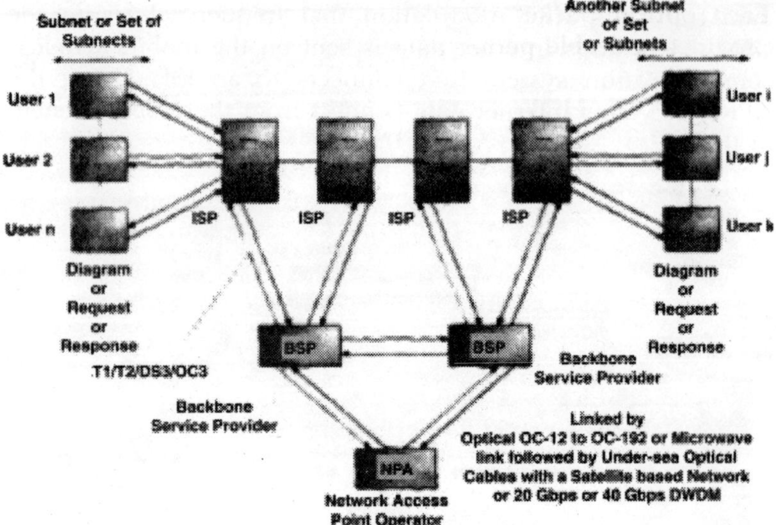

Fig. 1.2 : ISPs, Backbones and Network Access Point Operators.

There are also the Network Access Point Operators. These interconnect the Backbones at high or very high speeds. The connection is made through either the Synchronous Optical Network (SONET) OC-3C at 155 Mbps, or through the ATM switch connections using OC-12 (622 Mbps) fiber backbone, OC-48 (2.48832 Gbps), OC-192 at 9.953 Gbps, or through satellite links. Wavelength Division Multiplexing (WDM) has four windows:

(i) 1.4 mm,
(ii) 1.3-13.30 mm,
(iii) 1.530-1.565 mm (C-band),
(iv) 1.565-1.620 mm (Emerging L band).

Different windows can support the different protocols: Ethernet 10 Mbps, Ethernet 10 Gbps, ATM, IP, Frame Relays, etc. SDHK technology 20 Gbps and 40 Gbps optical communication are also feasible using Dense WDM (DWDM), in which there are optical packets instead of optical pulses.

Each optical packet supports a different protocol. DWDM provides scaleable performance.

5. HOW DOES A USER CONNECT TO THE INTERNET?

(i) To connect to the Internet, we must posses an appropriate host machine: a computer or terminal providing computer resources. A host machine can be a PC running Windows 95, Window 98, Windows NT, or Windows 2000; or a PC running Unix, Linux, or some other operating system. It can also be a Mac computer. A **socket** is an application layer interface between the two applications (software) on the local or remote computer. A socket forms a virtual circuit (connection) between two resources. A **WinSock** is a socket on Windows. It is a standard application-programming interface between the software running on Microsoft Windows and the TCP/IP and UDP-connected applications. A WinSock uses a driver, an application package for interfacing the Windows and TCP/IP protocols. Windows should have an appropriate WinSock driver for connecting the applications (software or files) to the Internet. A **datagram** (defined in Section 1.3) is a special type of data packet. A datagram can use as a User Datagram Protocol (UDP) for its transmission from a source to destination. UDP is a simpler protocol used for simple messaging applications. The UDP header has 16-bit source port-field that identifies the port number and a 16-bit destination port-field that identifies the server port number. It has 16-bit field for **length** (total number of words in the data after the header) and a 16-bit field for checksum. Header is followed by the 32 bit-words. The protocols have two classifications: connection-oriented and connectionless. A data resembles like a stream. If any data-packet becomes lost in a connection-oriented protocol, like, for example, an FTP, the message is retransmitted till successful and reliable transmission has been achieved. In a connectionless protocol, like UDP, the lost packet cannot be retrieved as sender and receiver do not track each and every packet. There is no sequence number. Examples of simple messages are message between a web server, mail server, or DNS and a computer system. A UDP message is broadcast from a source-host and all the other hosts listen. The targeted one responds. A TCP/IP message, on the other hand, establishes a point-to-point interconnection between a specific client and a specific server. Therefore, once a connection is established between the client and server Sockets by UDP, the HTTP requests and responses interchange using TCP/IP headers.

(ii) A user must have a modem that transmits and receives the data at 14.4 kbps, 28.8 kbps, 33 kbps, or 56 kbps. A modem at these four speeds uses a telephone line. A modem is a modulation-demodulation circuit. It converts bits from the computer into appropriate signals for the line and *vice versa.* The high-speed modems transmit on the line at the speed of 33 and 56 kbps. Let the 28.8 kbps and 56 kbps be the throughput of data bits from the 33 kbps and 64 kbps modems, respectively. The remaining 4 and 8 kbps channels are now available for the analog and digital telephone signals, respectively. For the voice signals, an analog voice transmission has an average frequency of 3.4 kbps. In digital telephony, the bits corresponding to the voice signals generate by taking the 8-bit samples taken every 125 ms to give the output at 8 kbps (= reciprocal of 125 ms). [A sample means finding the analog signal amplitude at an instance and converting it into the 8 bits using a converter].

(iii) We use the operating system, Windows or Linux or Unix. These posses a dial-up program that is integrated into and is available with the system. This program connects to the Internet and its services by dialing through the modem to the ISP. Our computer has then networks to the Internet. We can also get a dial-up software from an ISP. Once we connect, we get many other software free from the Internet by the FTP downloads.

(iv) We need a dial-up PPP account (or any other lower-end account—a SHELL account or a SLIP account) with our ISP.

There may be the several ISPs in a city. In India, there are the following: ISPS, Videsh Sanchar Nigam Limited (VSNL), Sancharnet, Satyam On-line, Mahanagar Telephone Nigam Ltd. (MTNL), Mantra, and Dishnet. There are also international gateways for the Internet and we could choose the one offering the best service in our city for our applications. In USA, the popular ISPs are America On-line (AOL) now tied up with Warner, Microsoft Network (MSN), Netcom On-line Communications, Computer Science, Prodigy and so on.

A dial-up means establishing a connection on dialing. A modem does the dialing. It uses a software (or embedded software) to connect to the Internet. [The embedded software is not on magnetic media (hard disk) or on optical media (CD). It is in the form of machine codes that are written for the embedded processors on an Electrically Programmable Device (EPLD)]. The connection can be a smart connection: this means that it possesses auto repeat-dialing and auto disconnect features. Thus, if connection is not made within a preset time, or if a line is idle for a preset time, or on completion of the specified tasks, the auto disconnect kicks into action. Moreover, its circuit may have wake-up features. The wake-up feature means that there is very low power dissipation when the computer is not in use, and activates only when called to use.

A PPP means Point-to-Point-Protocol A PPP account with an ISP supports access to all the Internet resources. It also provides a GUI that helps in Web browsing. Other accounts are as follows.

The Serial Line Internet Protocol (SLIP) is one that can carry only the TCP/IP. Like PPP, it also provides a GUI. However, the PPP supports many other protocols besides TCP/IP and is also usable over a variety of connections, for example, Novell Netware.

There is another account called SHELL account. It is different from a SLIP or PPP account. It is for the specific users of UNIX or LINUX. In SHELL, our computer dials and connects to a remote host computer that is on the Internet. It is like a login into the ISP computer without the TCP/IP or other protocol support. In PPP or SLIP, we login into our computer itself, not into that of the ISP.

We connect to the Internet using a modem and a dial-up PPP account. This facility has been available since 1992. Billing is done on an hourly basis, and the user can purchase 100, 250, or 500 hours in advance. The account will be continuously monitored and the hours of use debited. On completion, the user will have to purchase hours again. We, of course, also have to pay for the use of the telephone line to the telephone service provider.

Before signing up with an ISP, we must check its services. Questions to be asked are as follows :

(i) Does the ISP provide e-mail, FTP, Telnet, Internet Relay Chat, Usenet, and other popular utilities, VOIP, etc.?

(ii) Is each service to be accessed by a single concurrent login?

(iii) Is e-mail permissible using a personal e-mail address?

(iv) Does the ISP offer technical supports and services, for example, a 10 MB Web page for putting up a site? Technical support should be available with a call whenever there is problem with the connection.

(v) Does the ISP charge for technical services or are they available free of cost?

(vi) Does the ISP offer the requisite speed to support the modem speed?

(vii) Does the ISP possess sufficient incoming lines so that the user does not get a busy message very often?

(viii) How much memory storage does the ISP offer for our e-mails, etc.?

(ix) Does the ISP provide multiple dial-up numbers?

(x) Does the ISP provide Internet fax, Internet telephone access service, multicast networking, etc.?

(xi) Does the ISP provide WAIS, Gopher, Finger, Archie, Veronica, and other tools?

(xii) Does the ISP possess access numbers in other cities that the user can access when travelling?

(xiii) Does the ISP interconnect a WAP Gateway for access by cell phones?

(xiv) Does the ISP host and also interconnect CGIs, servlets, ASPs, and JSPs for dynamic responses from a website?

A computer with an appropriate operating system and software, a modem and a dial-up PPP or other account, with a suitable ISP, are the minimum requirements to become connected to the Internet.

ADDRESSES AND NAMES FOR THE INTERNET, WEB OBJECTS, AND SITES

Every country has a distinct country code, a city code, and local telephone number that enables us to connect to them on the telephone. How can we interconnect two objects, systems, and networks on the telephone without assigning these addresses and/or names?

There is a city. In the city there is a beautiful garden. In the garden there are many flowering plants. There are rose plants and there are deep maroon flowers. But there has to an appropriate addressing scheme to search for a beautiful, deep maroon-colored rose plant. To locate the rose we want, we specify first the city, then the garden, then the rose plants, and finally the deep marooned rose. Similarly, for an Internet resource access, there are standard ways of addressing and naming. Figures 2.3 (a) to (c) show the various ways of addressing and naming.

1. IP Address

How can we define a host on the Internet? A standard protocol (Section A.2.3) for Internet, IP has both the source and destination addresses. Each of these addresses is of four bytes. As each byte has 8 bits, there are four decimal numbers or hexadecimal numbers. Each number is between 0 and 255 decimals, i.e. 00H and FFH hexadecimals. An IP address is

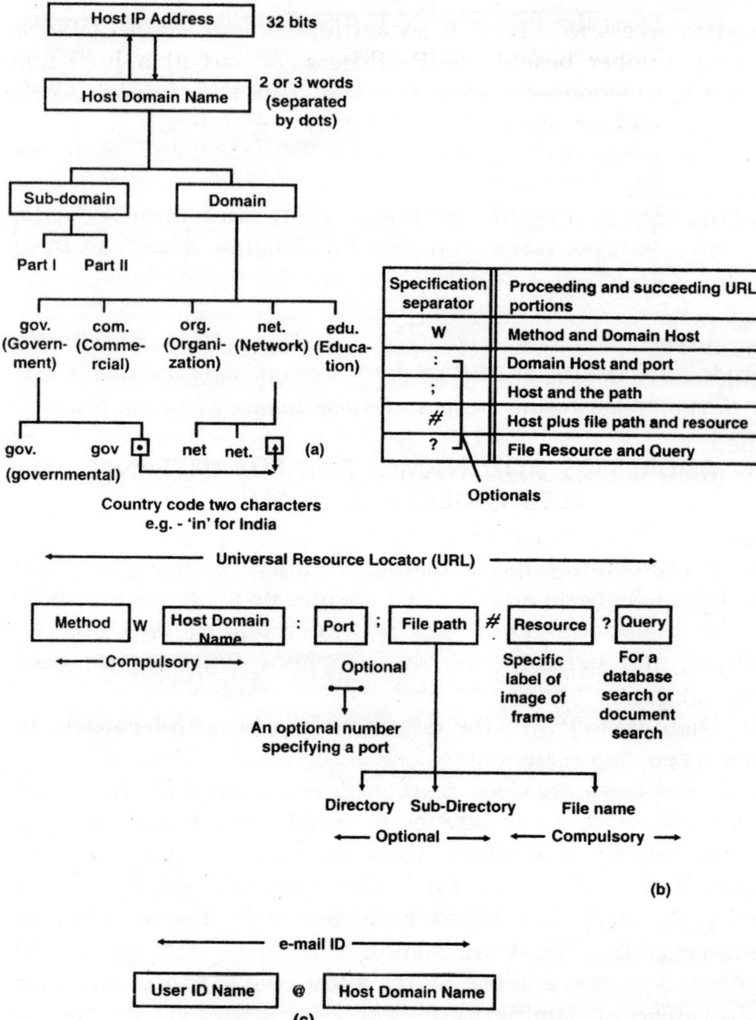

Fig. 1.3 (a) Domain Name format (b) The domain names format for an Internet user or host or for a Web (www) site, (b) URL addresses format for locating any web object, document, page, or data base on the Internet (c) E-mail address format for an individual or a group.

used to access to a port. A socket for network connection has a port number beside an IP address. A port at a host may direct the responses for the requests from the network to the multiple sockets (destination IP addresses and port numbers).

There are four numbers separated by a dot in-between. Hence an IP address is written as, for example, 150.80.0.231. Figure A.2.2 in Appendix A shows the IP address scheme. The message-packets from source to destination ISPs use an IP address by placing 32 bits according to the protocol in the packet header. The ISPs can assign static addresses to each source and destination. However, at the ISPs, a dynamic IP address can be generated in an instant to route a message.

The dynamically assigned IP addresses are very useful. These help in auto-handling messages between the ISPs when the traffic is large and the routes are few. The message packets from a user to the ISP or from an ISP to the destination uses the static IP addresses in the IP protocol. Each IP address used to connect between the user and the ISP has to be registered by paying a certain fee.

In order to manage the huge network traffic on the Internet, the network traffic routes use routers interconnecting the subnets.

How do we obtain media access when an Ethernet LAN connects to the Internet? How does an individual host with an IP address connect using the MAC address to access the media?

IP version 6 (IPv6) or IP next Generation (IPng) has now emerged for broadband Internet. In it there are 128-bit IP addresses instead of the 32-bit version of Ipv4. It has advanced data encryption and packet header features.

2. Domain Name Instead of an IP Address

How can we define a host on the Internet easily? The four-number IP address is difficult to recall by an individual or organization working on a host machine. A user of host machine thus uses a specific set of subdomain and domain names. Each name has a few alphanumeric characters. These are easier to recall compared to a four-number IP address. One example is 'ibm.com'. The subdomain name is 'ibm' and basic domain name is '.com'. Another example is **'bom4. vsnl. net**

in'. The **'bom4'**, **'vsnl'**, and **'net'** are the hierarchical subdomain names. The '.in' is the country-specific domain name (in this case, India). Another example is '.my', which is the country-specific domain name for Malaysia. On every use, the full domain name translates at the ISP to a four-number IP address and a meaningful connection is made between the user machine and the ISP. Instead of the IP protocol and IP address, it is possible to use another protocol called UDP to communicate the domain name from the user to the ISP, and use a port address scheme. There is a **look-up table** at the ISP. The IP address is taken from there for routing packets. [A look-up table is like the contents pages in any book. One can look into it to collect information]. The ISP also has a domain name system (DNS) that does the translation service through a look-up table. [An IP address from the look-up table may further be modified. A routing algorithm may generate a dynamic IP address. That is the address used between two routers. These routers are at the source and destination ISPs.] **Each domain name for the message packets between the user and ISP has to be registered (along with the corresponding IP address)** by paying a certain fee. **A web site on the World Wide Web is also registered by this scheme.**

How does one find the IP address of the destination and the in-between hops through the routers that forward the packets? Let us assume that we are using Windows. Now click **Start** and then **Run.** Type **Command Prompt.** An MS-DOS Window opens up. Type *tracert www.davv.ac.in.* The tracert utility provides IP addresses for the each router and the hops for the packets. What is the last IP address of the destination ***davv.ac.in?*** Repeat and run the utility tracert for other sites of interest.

3. Uniform Resource Locator (URL)

An object is a general term. It can mean a file, page, table, form, data base, audio clip, video clip, image, figure, document, etc. A form means a page(s) or sheet(s) with questions as well as associated spaces against each question for filling in the details. It is then converted into a database. The database is created from the information put-in by a candidate (or an applicant or sender). The candidate may be, enrolling in a course, registering with a web site to receive information, etc. It is difficult to locate (access) an object unless three things are well defined:

(i) A method of accessing and retrieving the object (For example an HTTP request and response),
(ii) A host (server) which is hosting the object, and
(iii) A path to the object's location.

Defining a URL is a standard method of locating an object on the Internet. It has an address format. A URL for the resources, pages and documents on the Web is as per an address format. Let us assume a nonexistent URL: *http://www.microsoft.coTn/msojfice/winword/inetchp2.htm* as an example for describing a URL.

First, we name a service. A service means a method for accessing the object by a request and for retrieving the object by a response. It also refers to a protocol for access to a host or a type of site in a URL. For example, *http://*indicates that the protocol HTTP is being used for service (to the Browser from the web server and *vice versa*). There are the colon and double slash after the service. Other examples are:

(a) ftp:// : The ftp:// defines the file transfer protocol for a file transfer (recall) service.
(b) telnet:// : The telnet:// defines the login service to the remote computer by the-dial up to the host computer.
(c) https://. This indicates that the method being used is the HTTPS: hypertext transfer protocol (HTTP) after authentication through the SSL layer.
(d) Other services are news, nntp, and mailto.

Second, we name a host. The host is defined just after the double slash. A host name means a sequence of characters specifying the type of site, subdomain, and domain. Each of these has a dot in between as a separator. For example, consider a host name, *www.microsoft.com*. The www before a dot (and after double slash for the service) means that site is the World Wide Web site. After a dot, 'microsoft' means that it is the subdomain name. After a dot, the 'com' stands for the domain of Commercial Organizations. If it were 'edu' instead of 'com' it would mean that the domain is that of Educational Institutions. If it were 'ac.in' instead of 'com' it would mean that the domain is Academic Institutions in India. In India, we also use 'ernet', meaning the domain of Educational and Research Network. This is a service provided by a government organization, the National Information Center (NIC).

Third, after the host name, we can optionally define the port. For example, *vsnl.com:* 80. We can define the host along with the port for the URL connection. Between port number and host, there is always a colon. The host name along with a port defines a socket for interconnection to another socket at the client's end. This is optional because, for example, *http://* itself implies that the port number should be 80. Therefore, when we connect to a web site, the port number is automatically inserted by the client browser.

Fourth, we optionally name a path. The **path** precedes a single slash after the host name. A path means a sequence of the folder and/or sub-folder and/or document. A single slash separates each of these in a path. For example, msoffice/winword/inetchap2.htm. The folder name is msoffice/winword: that is, msoffice that has the sub-folder winword. The sub-folder winword has a file inetchap2.htm, which stands for a document inetchp2.htm. The extension htm means an HTML document: the latter is in the hypertext document format, not in the txt or doc format. If only a slash occurs in the URL and not the path thereafter, it means that the browser accesses the complete directory holding the documents by the domain name. If no slash occurs in the URL and no the path thereafter, it means that the browser accesses the first page from a document that can be accessed by the domain name.

Fifth, we optionally name a **resource** at the document, that the path defines. The resource precedes a hash sign (#) after the path. A resource definition is like a bookmark on a page. It can be a labelled text, an image, or a frame on the page.

Sixth, we optionally define a **query** from the resource at the document. The query precedes a question-mark sign (?)

after the path or resource. A query definition is used for retrieving a specific search result from the resource.

4. The e-mail Address

How can we define a mail address unless two things, the individual name and the address are well defined? In an e-mail address, the host address is like a home or organizational address. It is definable by the domain name and the corresponding IP address for that host (the individual machine, LAN, or autonomous system). The e-mail address is thus similar to the domain name scheme with one difference, however. The address has to be for a specific individual or group of individuals and not for a host (specific machine or autonomous system).

We usually follow an Internet e-mail standard, RFC 822. Here the sign @ separates the individual identity with the Internet address in the domain name format. We pronounce @ as 'at the'. It is a procedure analogous to the sign :// (colon followed by double slash) which when it precedes the Internet domain name, separates the service definition. An example is *bala_phd2010@yahoo.co.in* The bala_phd2010 refers to the individual (this author). The user is registered at the subdomain 'yahoo' and domain 'com'. Another example is elexdavv@sancharnet.in. There is a 'School of Electronics' at the Devi Ahilya Manonmadian Sundaranar (University). The *sancharnet.in* is the subdomain and domain name for the Internet address registered the this school of studies for sending and receiving e-mail messages.

There is also another standard, European and Canadian. It originates from International Telecommunication Union-Telecommunications (ITU-T). Called X.400 it is used for e-mail services on the data networks. It allows the mailing of text and graphics, it can be used for faxes, and for data interchanges. The X.400 is since long period and the Internet e-mail standard, RFC 822. The former allows an inter-networking of the various e-mail systems.

We use the addresses and names for the services, e-mail messaging, web objects, and to access sites on the Internet. There are the standard ways of writing addresses that indicate the IP address, the domain name, the e-mail address, the URL and MAC address.

1. E-mail

Electronic mail or e-mail, as we all know it, is one of the most important services that has become possible because of the Internet. About 5% of all usage of the Internet is for e-mail messages. All over the world, there has been an e-mail revolution along with the Internet revolution. The only requirement for e-mail is that both sender and receiver have at least one account each for the e-mail service with their respective ISPs.

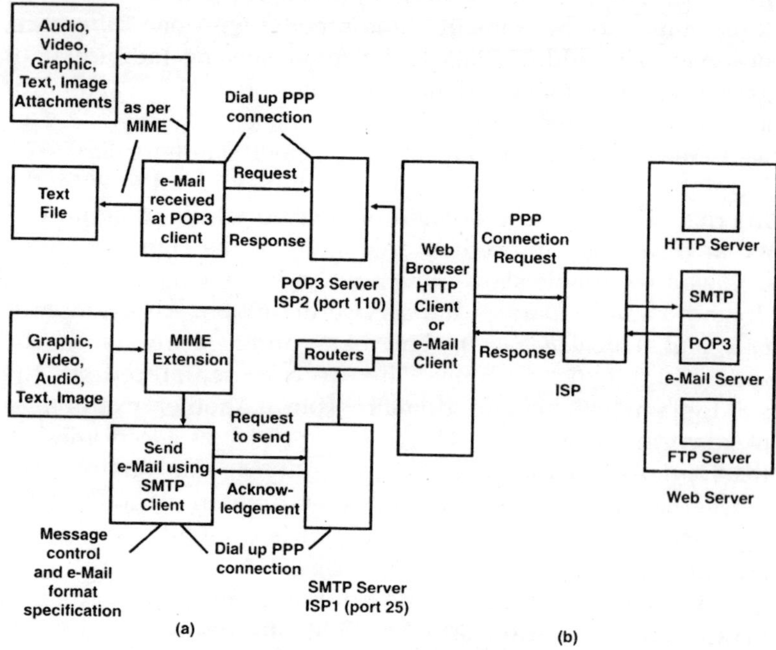

Fig. 1.4 : (a) The e-mail procedure when both sender and receiver usse the individual internet PPP account with an associated e-mail account. (b) The e-mail procedure when both sender and receiver use the Internet account of the other hosts. These hosts offer either free or paid e-mail accounts. The letter separate from the ISPs e-mail accounts.

(i) Both have to run their e-mail programs. [Note: A web browser may be using push technology. In that case, a web browser or itself will access the e-mail. No separate e-mail program is then needed].

(ii) Both use their individual e-mail addresses according to format

1. *The e-mail Process*

A sender (or someone) prepares a text, which is then transmitted via the Internet. A few clicks of the mouse will connect to the Internet and the mail is sent. This mail gets saved on an allocated storage space, which is assigned whenever an Internet address that resides at an ISP host is accessed. The receiver connects to the Internet, finds the e-mail waiting and a few clicks later, the message is downloaded and can be read. We must observe **Netiquette** during the e-mail drafting. Netiquette means an accepted behavior on the network during the e-mail, Usenet or chat. If there is a greeting, it must be reciprocated. Never swear on an Internet message. It is not ethical. Be kind to other views and emotions. Never key-in an offensive or flaming message. Think coolly before sending. Read coolly before a reply. Never be impolite.

In a matter of seconds, an e-mail message from one individual transmits to another individual. explains the procedure for the e-mail connection when the PPP account associated with the e-mail are used by both sender and receiver. Normally there is only one account for e-mail, which an ISP offers. In that case a sender and/or receiver can open the e-mail accounts with another host on the Internet. the user logins (connects) to a host web server through the HTTP service. The exemplary host web servers are 'http:// www.jaAoo.com', 'http://www.77z.rn.c07w" and *'http:// www.indiatimes.com'*. The user first connects to the website and then receives or sends a mail.

Some hosts like *yahoo.com, msn.com, indiatimes.com, hotmail.com, rediffmail.com, yahoo.com, mailcity.com,* etc. offer free e-mail accounts to attract individuals to their network or their advertisements. [One expects that the free facility will reduce in future.] To partly recover the cost of this free facility, the advertisements may be sent as an e-mail by these hosts. The registered addresses may be made available to another organization seeking that from the host. Before signing up with any of these free e-mail services, we should check which one provides fast access, sufficient storage space, and which push no advertisements or only, a limited number of advertisements.

2. *The Features and Services from the e-mail Programs*

Most e-mail programs nowadays offer the following features and services. We must note here that not all the following may be available in a particular e-mailing program. We must check these while using the program.

1. Off-line and On-line Text Drafting

We are able to prepare the text of the message off line. Off-line means disconnected from the Internet. It helps in saving costs when a connection time is charged. Off-line drafting lets one use the e-mail program of our own. For example, Outlook Express.

Beware! Off-line may not mean disconnected. No disconnection means ticking a telephone meter.

We are also able to prepare text message on-line. On-line means connected to the Internet. It is used when the connection charges are on a flat monthly or yearly basis. On-line drafting lets one use the e-mail program provided by the ISP.

2. Spell Check

Spell checking is essential before an e-mail message is ready. Even correction to a reply message which copies a part of text from the original mail, may also be programmable

3. Text Style Capabilities

A text for the e-mail may be in various styles like Times New Roman, Courier New, etc. It may be in various font sizes, 10 or 12 point, etc.

4. Expanded Text

An e-mail program may provide an expanded text feature that allows us to storé abbreviations, which are then automatically expanded when used. For example, NT can be abbreviation. It expands to Window NT 5.0. The stored abbreviations help us in quickly drafting an e-mail. In a business mail, for instance, we always type at the top of a mail the full name, address, pin code, telephone number, fax-number, e-mail address, etc. of the organization. If we store all this information as abbreviations it means that only a few characters need be typed, saving time and ensuring accuracy. The expanded text feature is a very useful feature of an e-mail program.

5. Clickable URLs

This is a sophisticated feature in certain e-mail programs, such as NetScape Messenger, Microsoft Outlook, etc. It provides a clickable URL in an e-mail. The receiver can click to a selected document in the Web. The Web Browser program opens up the page to which the URL points. These URLs may also be sent as attachments which are at the pointed Web pages by the URLs.

6. Aliases or Nicknaming

We can store abbreviated names which automatically expand to the full name with the e-mail address in a field named **To: field.** The To: field is an area on the screen. Here we must specify the e-mail address. This facility differs from expanded text. The expanded text feature is for use anywhere during drafting. The nickname feature is for use only in the To: field. [A field is a part of a screen, some allocated display space or a keying in space for a string of characters. There are also From: field and Subject: field].

7. Encoding Colours on the Message Labels

Sometimes, in order to attract the attention of the reader to a specific part of the text, we may highlight the text in some way. For example, a warning can be in red. The subject field may be in maroon. The detailed matter may be in blue, and so on. We can label the message with different colours in different sections, parts or sub-parts. This encoding feature helps in this task.

8. Appending Signature or Business Card

We may like that a signature or business card *automatically appends* at the end (or top) of an every out box mail. The signature may mean all these, a sender name, designation, company, phone-number, fax-number, e-mail address, URL for sender's Web page, etc.

9. Draft Save and Text Save

A good letter takes time to write. A draft is an incomplete message. We also have to keep our message brief, to the point and in short paragraphs. We may have to reconsider improper-words. We have to think of e-mail ethics. We have to think of observing rules for polite interaction. We have to follow social norms. We have to delete, and not send any sensitive material by e-mail. We have to think of not misquoting from another e-mail. We have to think of mentioning the subject and earlier references properly. Therefore, an e-mail message composition takes time. It has to be drafted appropriately. An e-mail program may provide for a file or folder, which stores the draft stage of a letter or message. We can then recall it to complete. Only the final text is sent and saved in an appropriate file.

10. Attachments with the e-mail

This is an important feature offered by many e-mail programs, such as Outlook Express 2000, NetScape messenger, Microsoft Outlook, etc. We first call a utility for a new message and key in our message. We then click to Attach utility. We choose the file from the dialog box. Here the receiver gets the file attached to the e-mail. We then click the message save button. When we click a button, send, for sending this message, then that chosen file also transfers with the message. This feature is different from the clickable URL feature in an e-mail where the recipient connects to a Web page on a click. In this case, the recipient gets a file with the message.

11. Messaging (and) Application Programs Interface (MAPI)

This feature helps the sender to create a message in a special way. While keying in the message, a MAPI compliant file can be selected and attached. For example, if we require a table to be attached MAPI helps in attaching that to a message.

12. Voice Recording for an e-mail Attachment

This feature helps in recording a voice or audio message and sending it as an e-mail attachment.

13. Send e-mail

The e-mail program has a send utility. We click the send button after specifying a file in the **From:** field. The file is the one where the mail is. To: field specifies where to send the message. There is usually an OutBox feature. An OutBox is where all the outgoing messages are stored.

14. Scheduling Delivery Date and Time

This feature helps in scheduling the delivery date and time for the messages in the outbox. It helps in sending the messages all at one time may be when the connection or line charges are low. Suppose dialing to an ISP is free between 10 P.M. and 5 A.M. we can then schedule sending out box messages for that time. For example, consider birthday (or festival day) greetings. These also need to be scheduled on specific date at morning time.

15. The e-mail Inbox Wait Message

An e-mail program may have an inbox or mailbox feature. An **inbox** or **mailbox** is where all the incoming messages are automatically stored, so that the receiver can look at these later.

When we enter our home, we check our mail in the *pigeon hole* (Mail Box) from post office. Similarly, when we connect on Internet, the e-mail program begins by an automatic display. In some e-mail programs we may have to click an appropriate icon to display the inbox contents or for just arrived messages. The inbox shows the From: field, Subject: field, day, date, time, etc. It may also display the total number of unread messages.

[The **From:** field is for the sender's e-mail address. The **Subject:** field is for the subject of the e-mail. Examples of a subject are 'New Year Greeting' or 'Top Job For You', etc. The field, for the Day, Date and Time, is for specifying the day, date and time of the e-mail message.]

16. Poll Timing Set

This feature enables us to preset the time or time periods for a day or week. It then automatically scans the Internet for new mail. Of course there must be a connection to the Internet at that time

17. The e-mail Alerts

Let us assume that we have a new mail. But we are disconnected to the Internet. This feature in an e-mail program helps us to get an audio tone or a visual alert. The e-mail alert program runs in background. It runs just like a time display program when we run an application like Word.

18. Reading Mails

Once the inbox shows the lists of messages waiting to be read, we double click on a message. The message opens in full in a window on the screen. After working with that, we return to the inbox and read the other mail. We can read mail on-line or off-line. On-line means while connected to the Internet. Off-line means while disconnected. It means after storing the message from the Internet.

19. Reminder

The feature is used to remind ourselves of a fixed date and time. This feature helps us in sending and scheduling our mails. These messages from the outbox give the reminder messages in the inbox of same destination as the source on the scheduled dates and times.

20. Compressing the In-Box Mails Space

This feature helps us in freeing disk space when we delete the multiple folders of in mail messages.

21. Compressing an e-mail Attachment

An e-mail may have long text, voice, images, and video that have to be in the compressed format for sending and for receiving. A modulation technique called Adaptive Differential Pulse Code Modulation (ADPCM) is used. A compression format for voice message is as per ITU recommended standard. It can also be a compression standard called Global System for the Mobile-Telephone Communications (GSM). G.273 is another ITU recommended standard for the video conferencing, PC telephony, on-demand video and audio, and Internet-phone messages. Further, an e-mail may have graphics, images and video as attachments. A Web Browser may help in getting an image only in **.jpg** and **.gif** formats, (.gif stands for Graphic Interchange format).gif exists for a graphic, fax and mono colour figure. The 'jpg' is from an international compression standard by the Joint Photographic Expert Group **(JPEG).** For video data, the Moving Picture Expert Group's (MPEG), .mpg is the compression standard. The 'mp3' is a MPEG standard for video compression. NetScape uses the JPEG image display attachments.

22. Storing the In-box Mails

To save costs, we should just store a message at the in-box quickly. The message should be read after disconnecting from the Internet.

23. Mail Box Managing

This feature helps in creating a number of file folders. These folders have the messages arranged date-wise, sender identity-wise and subject-wise.

24. Deleting a Mail

To delete a message, we highlight the file folder or message and click the **Delete** tool. This feature helps in discarding received mail from the mailbox file folders. There may be a Trash Box (or recycle bin) feature. A Trash Box is where all the discarded messages can be stored automatically, and they remain there till completely removed.

25. Removing Expired Messages

This feature helps to automatically delete a message in case it has been read and is older than a preset number of days, say 30, 60 or 90 days.

26. Reply to an Incoming Mail

There is an icon for a command in the e-mail program that allows us to reply to an incoming message. This command opens a message space on the screen Inbox addressed back to the sender with the incoming message also displayed. This happens by an interchange of the **From** and **To** fields. [The **Subject** field does not change.] We can then reply easily by quoting a part or paragraph or subject from the previously open message.

27. Reply to All

There is a Reply to All feature in e-mail programs. Our reply is sent to all addresses the in-box.

28. Forwarding a Mail

This feature helps in redirecting an e-mail to another address or account.

29. Auto-forwarding a Mail

The auto-forward feature redirects the mail automatically to another e-mail address. There is an option to retain a copy of each auto-forwarded mail. For example, we are on vacation from our organization. We may then like someone else to attend to our mails. This person is a temporary substitute for us to reply to and attend to the mails in our absence.

30. Default Routing a Mail

This feature helps in specifying the default address when there are the multiple e-mail addresses for a person. All mail at any of the multiple addresses is routed to this default address automatically. This helps in routing messages in multiple in-boxes into a single inbox.

31. Automated Response

There is an automated response feature for replying to the all or selected addresses. It sends a certain message of the recipient automatically. The message may be information about vacation period or a thank you mail. The recipient message is sent automatically to all or selected addresses in the in-box. The recipient can also program to have the e-mails received from the specified e-mail addresses checked at scheduled times.

32. Mailing Lists

This feature helps in creating a master mailing list or contact group. When we recall this mailing list, it helps in selecting where to send a message. For example, the addresses where New Year greetings have to be sent can be selected. Using this list saves our time in keying the e-mail addresses repeatedly in the To Field at the time of sending a mail.

33. Exceptions

This feature helps in creating exceptions to certain e-mail addresses from a mailing list. When we recall a mailing list, it helps in not selecting those addresses to which the message should not be sent.

34. Nested Mailing List

This feature helps in creating the sub-lists in a master mailing list. We first recall a mailing list. We then select another mailing list from within it (a sub-list). From that list, we may again select another mailing list. This feature helps us in selecting specific addresses in a fashion similar to selecting a file folder. When a file is to be located and selected, we first select a directory, then another directory, then a sub-directory, and so on. Finally, from the last selected directory, we select a file. Similarly, there can be nested mailing lists. A use of the nested mailing list saves time in searching from one big list.

35. Distribution Lists

This feature helps in creating a distribution mailing list. A distribution list can be maintained for specific messages, e.g. New Year Greetings. Distribution lists, like all other mailing lists, saves time. An individual or a company can maintain multiple distribution lists.

36. Clickable Addresses for Mailing

If a message has to be sent to only certain specified addresses, there is an automated feature for selecting them. Whenever we use the message composing utility in the e-mail program, the addresses from a mailing list appear. By clicking on specific addresses, a message can be automatically sent to the clicked address or addresses.

37. Filters

We may like to specify certain criteria for identification of the incoming mail. If the incoming messages satisfy that criteria, they are filtered in and rest discarded. We can define criteria for filtering which can be based on And, Or, or Not logic. For example, we may specify key words. If the subject of e-mail has those key words then that mail can be filtered in and the rest discarded.

38. Multiple Accounts Managing

This feature helps a recipient to have and manage multiple e-mail accounts. Certain special keys called **hot keys.** These hot keys help in switching from one account to another for attending to incoming mail in each of these accounts. The messages in each of these accounts are treated differently. For example, the messages in some are to be saved; some to be responded to automatically, some forwarded automatically and so on.

39. Incremental Mailing

This feature helps in breaking a master mailing list into the sub-lists. A sub-list is a collection of addresses to which specific messages can be targeted. The message is then sent to addresses in each sub-list incrementally. There are thus multiple distribution lists, each used one by one. This helps in speedy transmission through the Internet

40. Integrating e-mail with Voice Mail and Fax

This is a sophisticated feature available in a select few

e-mail programs. It integrates e-mail with voice mail and fax. The e-mail program then

(i) supports the Multipurpose Internet Mail Extension (MIME) type files, and
(ii) sends the file with the extensions as an attachment. MIME Types are the file format descriptions. MIME is an RFC 1341 standard and from 1996, an RFC 2049 standard. It helps in integrating a text with voice, fax, image, and video. This integrates voice mail with text mail. A scanner scans a fax. The e-mail program then sends an image attachment in **.gif** format to the server. The other attachment formats are **.htm** or **.jpg** or **gif.** A format is in **.pdf** format if it uses Adobe Acrobat Reader as a plug-in. [A plug-in is a software that associates when needed by an application. It loads and executes when called to do so by the application software.] The extension htm or jpg or gif is then the first packet of the Internet message to the server (or client). The Client (Receiver) also reads the MIME types in an e-mail and searches for the required plug-ins at the receiver end for execution. An extension is a first packet in an interchange message. A program at the receiver's end identifies a file type from the extension received. Mime extension types are the standard ones. For example, a Word document is identified by the .doc file extension. An audio/voice recorder records in .wav format. A recorded voice has an extension file.wav (Windows Audio/Voice Format for mono or stereo/8 or 16 bit samples). Alternatively, a Windows-based software for a fax has to be used if the MIME type integration does not exist.

41. Wireless e-mailing

This is a sophisticated feature in a select few e-mail programs. It uses service Gateways like RadioMail. It helps in directing a short e-mail text to a pager. Radio Modem-connected computers can also be used for the wireless e-mailing.

3. *E-mail Programs*

Many e-mail programs exist that offer many of the features and services mentioned in NetScape and Microsoft are the leaders in Internet-related programs and brows-ers. NetScape Messenger is a part of the NetScape Communication Suite. [A communication suite is complete package for communication.] It has been prepared by NetScape Communications Corporation. NetScape Messenger is the e-mail component. NETCOMplete suite is another all-in-one package for the Internet. It has NETCOMplete Mail software in it for e-mail service. NetScape package runs under Microsoft Windows as well as X Windows. [X Windows are the Unix-based versions with Windows-like features.] NETcetera for Windows can be downloaded from *'ftp://ftp.airtime.co.uk/pub/ window/ netcetera/*

Microsoft Internet Explorer 5 suite has a software, Outlook, for e-mail. The Microsoft Internet Explorer website is *http://www.microsoft/ie.* The latest version e-mail program can be downloaded from the site. Microsoft Mail was used before the Window 95. Microsoft Exchange was used earlier with the Window 95 operating system. With Office 2000 now, the Outlook 2000 e-mail program is used.

4. *Protocols for E-mail on Internet*

Post Office Protocol (POP) is a protocol used for receiving e-mail. POP3 is the new version of this protocol. POP3 Client means a program used for receiving e-mail from a POP3 Server at an ISP. A user simply dials and accesses the e-mail server to get the mail. It is a request and retrieve (client requests and retrieves from the server)-based protocol.

Internet Message Access Protocol version 4 (IMAP4) , is the latest new standard in place of POP3. IMAP4 permits the following.

(a) Message status flags to indicate whether the message has been deleted (read) or answered.

(b) Three modes: On-line, off-line, and disconnect network-modes. Disconnect mode helps in synchronizing the connection.

(c) Concurrent access to a common mail box at the server.
(d) Allows mail to be received and sent simultaneously.
(e) Management of multiple mail boxes by a user. This helps in listing, renaming, creating, and deleting the received and deleted (read) e-mails into different folders. It enables the client to view from the IMAP server the heading and the sender's name to decide whether the message should be downloaded. Internet Group Message Protocol (IGMP) and Internet Control Message Protocol (ICMP) are two other protocols.

Another protocol is Simple Mail Transfer Protocol (SMTP). It is a standard protocol on the Internet for mail transfer. It specifies the e-mail format. It also provides for control of messages. For example, 'Retrieve short mail below 2 kb only' can be a control message; or, 'Retrieve festival-related mail only' can be another control message. SMTP headers are as follows; **mailfrom, rcptto, To:, CC:, bcc:** (for mailing the copies of messages to those not included in the original message), **Sender:, Subject:, Date:, Keywords:, Comment:, From: and Reply_To:** .

Another new protocol is ESTMP in place of SMTP. It permits pipelining of the messages so that transmission of multiple message commands simultaneously becomes possible. It has checkpoints within messages. This helps in easy re-transmission of an interrupted message. If a message is interrupted, the re-transmission occurs from the check-point only. Authentication is an important feature in ESMTP. It thus permits e-mail on the LAN as well as on the Internet.

5. Web Features

The World Wide Web is a continuously expanding large collection of hypertext documents. This collection now forms a grand—the Internet over the globe. A document has one or more pages. A page links to another page by a URL. The Home Page is the first page that has URLs to the subsequent pages in a document. An individual web site may have multiple documents. Website service is presently the most important service. It has currently about 45% usage of the Internet. There has been an Internet revolution because of the W'eb. It is creating social change in the way people interact with each other. It is changing the way in which we get information. It provides an information superhighway.

The Web has unique features:

(i) It is a grand globally distributed Internet service.
(ii) It is platform independent. (A platform means a specific computer system, say, Pentium III with an operating system like Windows 98).
(iii) It has GUI features with easy navigability through hypertext and multimedia links
(iv) It is interactive, because of search engines, push technology features like Web casting, etc. [Refer to Sections 5.6 and 7.]
(v) It is continuously expandable and is updated almost by the minute.

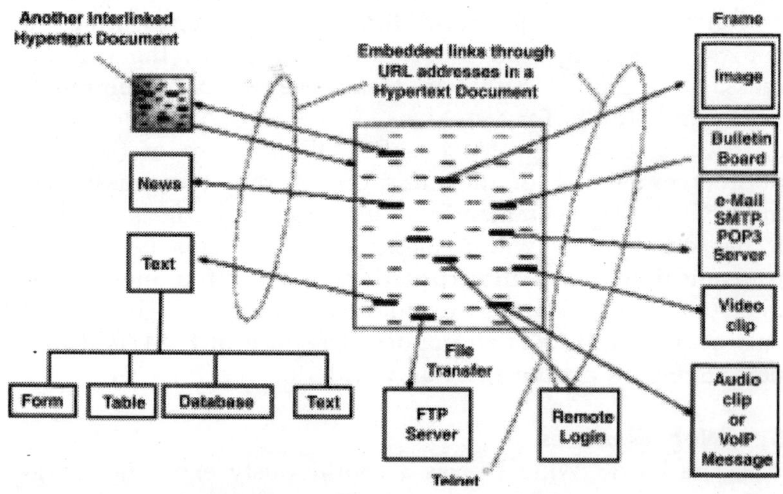

Fig. 1.5 : A hypertext document. [The World Wide Web is a large collection of such documents, known as the web pages. A collection of interlinked pages and documents forms a website.

(vi) By processing the web contents, using CGI, Servlets, JavaScript, ASP, or JSP the services for e-mail, e-com, and m-com are also feasible.

6. The Hypertext Document

(i) A hypertext document ties together information from multiple sources (URLs). A resource can be the following or a section of the following :

(a) Another Web page.
(b) File Transfer.
(c) Telnet.
(d) Index.
(e) Table.
(f) Form.
(g) Image.
(h) Voice (or music) clip.
(i) Video clip.
(j) News
(k) Gopher, etc.

A hypertext document has text along with links (branches and labels). Each link is defined by a URL address. Each link is either underlined or is in a colour different from that of the text. [The colours of a used and an unused link may also differ.] A click at the link readily leads us to another local or remote resource. An important feature of a link is that it provides a sequential as well as nonlinear method to read a page or resource. An example of sequential link is the pages of a textbook. An example of a nonlinear link is the contents pages or index pages of a book.

(ii) We use a language Hyper-Text Mark-Up Language (HTML) to prepare the hypertextdocument page for the static functionality.

(iii) When embedded in an HTML document are the programmable features using the Scripts, Servlets and COMs, the dynamic functionality imbibes, the pages create dynamically create and the DHTML features imbibe.

(iv) A HTML document can be browsed and downloaded using a corresponding Browser for it. the Browsers for the HTML documents at the web sites in detail.

(v) A resource is accessed by an HTTP request to a web server that hosts the resource.

A hypertext document thus has not only the text but also provides the images, audio, and video. While pointing to a word in a textbook, we cannot get an audio clip. But by pointing and clicking to a link in a hypertext document, we can have access to audio, video and so on. A link leads us to a URL. At the URL, there may be an another text document pointing to other URLs for the texts and databases, tables, forms, etc. At the URL page, there may be a text document pointing to video clips, voice (or music) clip, figures, graphs, photographs, e-mail service, FTP service, other services on the Internet, even to other URLs, etc. Using a hypertextdocument, we can navigate (search, share, search and copy, transfer) back and forth. We thus go through the documents and pages stored at many addresses. A click at a URL is like looking into a page using the index at the end of a book whenever the reader finds a new term that he wants to know more about. The only difference is that here, not only does the reader get the text by a click on the URL but also the images, files, etc.

A website host-address is shown in explains the URL addresses. The World Wide Web is a grand collection of web sites. A web site has a text along with collection of linked URLs.

A hypertext is a text document with links. The links are made through URLs and SRCs (sourcing a resource on call) that are pointers to another page or resource. A link may be link for a new page, a new picture, to initiate sending mail, or to execute a program. The links are very important since they act like glue to hold all the web pages together along with the resources that could be the other web sites, files, images, data bases, tables, forms, services, etc.

7. Document and Web Access Using WAP

Can we access the web with only a web Browser or are there new revolutionary devices going to be available in the future? For example, **Web Companion** is a new device. [It is of the size about a text book.] It runs on **Windows CE,** an embedded operating system from Microsoft. What will be the advantages? It will make it possible for us to access a web site, using the Internet connection. But the Internet access are now not only be from a PC but also from Internet compliant appliances, cellular phones, wireless personal digital assistants (PDAs), etc. [A PDA can receive the personal instructions, messages and data from the user. The user sends the messages to PDA using a cell phone, dial up Internet or wireless Internet. It then runs the application software on a native computer attached with it. It can also transmit the results and data to the user at remote location through Internet or wireless.] We can access the web not only with a web-browser but also using a new revolutionary wireless concept, Wireless Application Protocol (WAP) instead of HTTP.WAP lets cellular phones and PDAs facilitate this. It makes an Internet access possible from every room in an organization or home.

8. Using the Web Services and Web Browsers

A **Web Server** is a server that provides web and Internet services. The web server is also called a host for the websites (including URLs) and Internet services. The Web is based on the worldwide collection of hosts. These hosts are interconnected by routers. The ISPs provide the Web services and the Web servers.

A host may offer rent-paid websites. Each paid website has the memory space according to contract. A huge number of big as well as small organizations, universities, individuals, companies, government organizations possess their individual web sites. Each site generally has detailed information, messages, lessons, databases, forms, etc. A registered owner may continuously modify the site. We should check which host provides faster access through its web servers. We must also check whether the server provides sufficient storage space at a reasonable registration fee and annual fees. A host has a large number of registered users and registered sites.

Many hosts offer free web sites all over the world. These are *rediff.com, yahoo.com, hotmail.com, mailcity.com, itgo.com,* etc. Each free site has however only a limited memory space (5 MB or 10 MB). It is to attract the individuals to view the advertisements. It enhances the use of a specific telephone service or communication channel. These advertisements and the commission by the service channel generate revenue for the free hosting sites. These two sources of revenue compensate the cost of providing free website space. [Also popularly called a revolutionary model 'dot com'. The free e-mail, free website and free e-commerce, auction or other services by the dot com companies are the part of this model. These advertisements are invariably sent along with the web pages through these hosts. We should check which server provides faster web access and sufficient free storage space with little or no advertisements.

To access the Web, the requirements are that we have a PPP account with an appropriate ISP and a Web **Browser.** A front-end tool is a software to be used first. Later on, we can use all the utilities and applications provided in that software. A Windows operating system is an example of a front-end tool that leads to all the application software in a computer. Similarly, a web browser is a front-end tool. It is very easy to

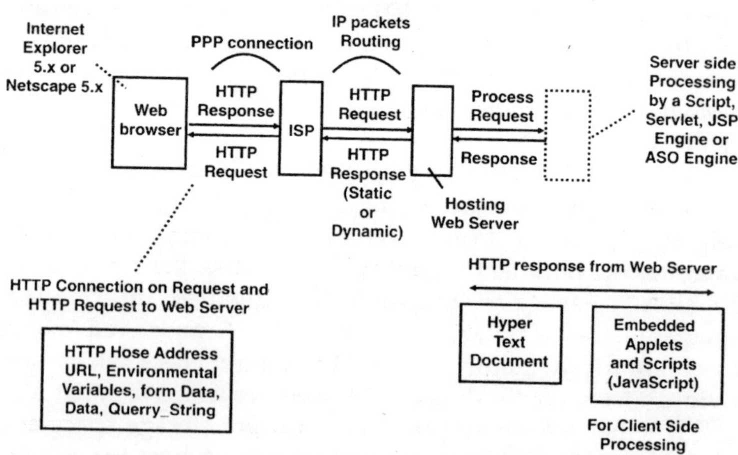

Fig. 1.6 : The Procedure for the Web Access.

use, to access web sites and to avail Internet services. It is the most widely used client software in the world. This is because of a unique graphic user interface (GUI) feature of the hypertext links.

There are other globally popular application suites. One is NetScape Communicator 4.5. and its recent version Netscape 5.x. Another is Internet Explorer 4 or its recent version IE 5.x. The third is Mosaic. Sections 3.5 and 3.6 describe the NetScape Communicator suite and Internet Explorer, respectively. Each of these application suites has a web browser as an integral and important part.

Transactions Server (or WAP Proxy Server or WAP Gateway), the HTML to WML and WML to HTML conversions occur.

Can we use HTTP service for an e-mail service or an FTP service? Yes, Protocol tunneling is such a technique. Recall Figure 2.4b for the e-mail service by this service. A connection can be made by HTTP but the message is transmitted using SMTP or FTP. An SMTP or FTP header and message parts are encapsulated within the HTTP header and message.

Let us assume that a university has an examination form on the Web. The form is an input to the user (candidate). Now the user fills the form online, while connected to the Internet. The form is processed at the website server after connecting to another server at the university. A CGI Script in PERL (Practical Extraction and Reporting Language) language scans a text and prints reports after appropriate formatting. [PERL has powerful operators instead of regular expressions. It is thus highly concise. It has a common and important application. The PERL program can process a hypertext

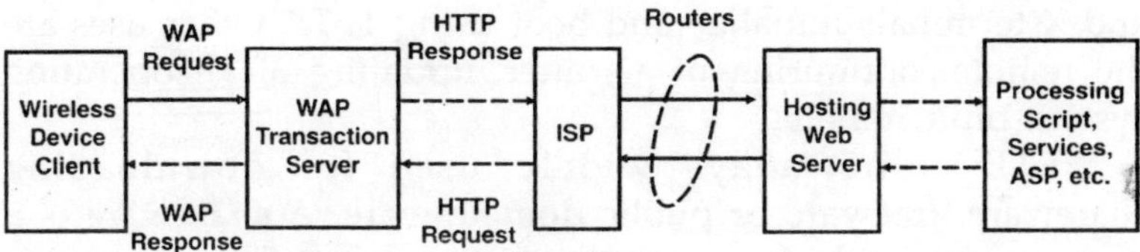

Fig. 1.7 : Wireless Application Protocol (WAP)-based Access Techniques.

documented form input if the program is hosted at the site through a FTP. PHP 4 is another pre-hypertext processor language. Refer to Sections 10.3.1 and 2 for details about the PERL and PHP.] At the browser side, the commonly used scripts are Scripts [JavaScript or JScript] A Script introduces the DHTML features also.

9. File Transfer

1. *File Transfer Features*

How do we upload the hypertext files from a web site into our computer or into a web server? How do we upload into the server Java applets? How do we upload the CGI (Common Gateway Interface) scripts? How do we send attachments with an e-mail? All this is done through a protocol-observing software. The protocol is called File Transfer Protocol (FTP).

A host computer program is called a FTP server when the server or host is the one that uses the **FTP** for transferring files to a client. A FTP *client is* then a user program that downloads a file from the server. The FTP is a part of TCP/IP application suite. A file, may be for the tutorial on a topic, information, data or script. A file may be a text file, hypertext document, database file, etc.

Instead of FTP another protocol can be used. It is called Trivial File Transfer Protocol (TFTP). It is used for the files without a folder (directory) or a sub-folder (file list). It is part of the User Datagram Protocol (UDP). UDP is less complex than TCP/IP. That is why the UDP is used by the DNS. What are the uses of TFTP? Few important uses are initializing and booting. The servers, disk-less computers, network computers and X terminals initialize and boot using TFTP. Other uses are the remote-configuring of a router, updating of an operating system on a remote.

FTP is nowadays widely used for downloading shareware, freeware or public domain-ware. A **shareware** is a program available free on an open resource. The resource is accessed generally through the Internet. There may be a few conditions for the user. Alternatively, there may be a license fee. A **freeware** is a shareware without any condition or license

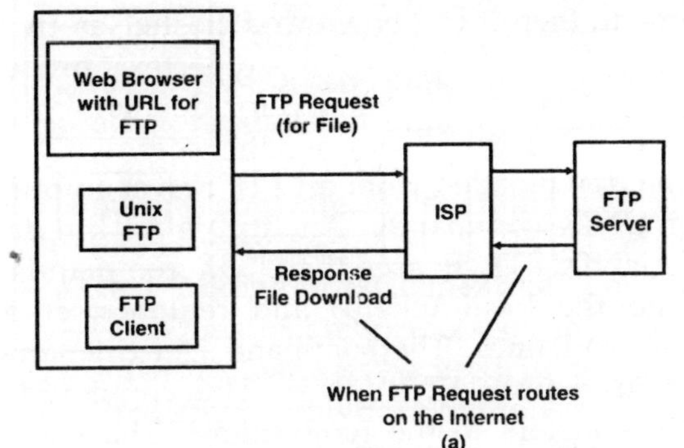

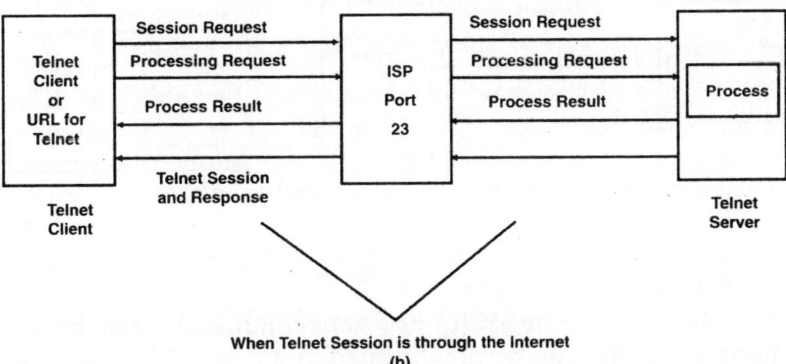

Fig. 1.8 : (a) An FTP session, (b) A Telnet Session.

fee. **Public domain** means that there is no copyright protection. Any one can use as well as distribute the product. There is no condition or fee, etc. Locations of available FTP programs are available at *http://www.tucows.com/*.

2. *File Transfer Services and Programs*

We need the following services for a file transfer :

1. *Web Browser for the FTP*

A file may be downloaded by using the web browser which links to an FTP server through a URL. the sequential ways in an URL for the download on a click at a link. The file can then be saved on our computer. Alternatively, if it is a hypertext document, then it can be viewed on the screen while browsing.

2. *UNIX-FTP*

A file can be downloaded from an FTP server to our own computer using UNIX commands. An **'ftp'** is an interface, a software for the UNIX FTP. It uses the UNIX commands. The interface between the local (client) and remote (server) is through the command lines. The command 'get (filename)' is for transfers from remote FTP server. The command 'put (filename)' is for transfers to the remote host. The command 'close' is for closing the UNIX session. The command 'quit' disconnects us from the remote server.

3. *Set of Files through the FTP*

A set of files may be downloaded (for the application); for example, an application suite at the **FTP server** on the Internet. For example, we use a UNIX command 'mput (filenames)'. This command transfers (a group of files) from the remote FTP server.

4. *FTP Client Programs*

There is no need to use the command lines-based interface. A file can be downloaded from the FTP server by using the FTP client. An FTP client is a dedicated program used for the file transfer in place of the web browser. The FTP client is a part of Windows 98 plus. Alternatively, we use an FTP client which is an on-line resource that provides GUI drag-and-drop-features. At an FTP client there are two partitions: one for defining a local file for the transfer and the other for defining a remote file to which the transfer takes place. At the partitions, there is a separate **field.** This field defines the local FTP client and for the remote server. Also there is a separate **window** for defining the directory that has been selected (e.g., A:, C:, D:, E:). There is a separate **window** for defining the file selected for receiving and serving the downloaded files, respectively.

Examples of the FTP clients are as follows:

(1) **WS_FTP** : One example of the FTP client on-line

resource is **WS_FTP.** It possesses features that are the same as that of Windows. Its latest version is from a web site of *Ipswitch*. The web site is at *http:// www.ipswitch.com/Products/ WS_FTP/ index.html.* It is a shareware. Its software engineer is John A. Junod. WS_FTP Pro 6.0 is a 1999 version. It is not a shareware. Its utility pact includes the following features: (*i*) Find, (*ii*) Script *(Hi)* Synchronize, (*iv*) Site Manager, (*v*) Quick Connect, (*vi*) Recursive delete to authorized user, (*vii*) Drag-and-Drop feature of Windows. [A Drag is an action from a server and a Drop is made to a client computer, folder or application.], (*viii*) Hosting of the FTP site and an FTP server for the other remote clients, (*ix*) *A* firewall support, (*x*) Integration with Explorer, (*xi*) Remote-to-remote transfer support, (*xii*) Ability to create a shortcut button clicking on which can start FTP or execute a batch of file commands.

(2) **CuteFTP** : Another example is **CuteFTP.** Its additional features are as follows. (*i*) It has resume feature on interruption. For long files, interruptions need this feature, (*ii*) It can list all file folders that were visited. It has also separate list for frequently visited file folders. (*iii*) It has default defining feature at the server as well as client for a frequently visited file folder and frequent user, respectively. It is a freeware for a limited period, only during the demonstration phase.

3. *File Formats, Use-Types and Transfer-Types*

A file uses a format that is either an **ASCII** or binary. A use-type is mostly recognized by an extension. The extension name is placed after a dot. There are numerous examples:

1. '.txt' for ASCII format text file.
2. '.htm' or '.html' for hypertext file.
3. '.com' for the executable binary file. [Remember '.com' for a file name and '.com' for a web site have the different meanings. The latter refers to a storage space allocated at a web server. It can be seen as part

of a URL address. Hypertext documents are stored in that location].

4. '.exe' for executable binary file.
5. '.zip' for a zip file. [A zip file is a compressed file which saves storage space and which can be expanded later by a program for unzipping. The popular programs for zip and unzip are pkzip and pkunzip.] '.z' for a UNIX zip file.
6. '.doc' for a Word file created by MSOFFICE binary.
7. '.pi' for a PERL (Practical Extraction and Reporting Language) program. We have the following types of the FTPs.

1. *Anonymous FTP*

We login to a remote computer through a UNIX command ftp. When asked we type in an anonymous user name and for a password, we type our e-mail address on the Internet. But if it is an anonymous ftp service, then what is the advantage of giving the e-mail address? It helps. The remote user can provide messages later, whenever there is a new version of the transferred file or whenever there is virus information to be passed on. Alternatively, we have an anonymous FTP through a web browser or through a URL for the anonymous FTP server.

Anonymous FTP is used for the transfer of shareware, freeware and public domain files. For the anonymous file transfer, TFTP can also be used instead of FTP because TFTP does not have authorization features like password, etc.

2. *Non-Anonymous FTP*

Non-Anonymous FTP is used for the transfer of files other than the shareware, freeware and public domain files. The user-name has to be supplied and it must have the authority to access the Non-Anonymous FTP server. The password is asked for by the server after it identifies the user. When the server identifies the user and finds the password to be correct, then the service can be accessed. In UNIX, the password is case sensitive. It may have the multiple case characters and numbers. What is the advantage of Non-Anonymous FTP? It helps. The remote server provides files only to authorized users. Authorization may be granted to a user for a limited period by paying a fee.

How do we download a configuration file? A configuration file may be for four messages: an ISP address, ISP gateway address, domain name, and Subnet mask. Instead of FTP, we use another protocol called BOOTP. It is a Bootstrap Protocol. It is part of IP/UDP.

4. *FTP URLs*

Table 1.1 gives the five ways of defining a URL for the FTP service when it is mediated by a web browser. A sequential URL address is written in the given in the successive columns of Table 1.1. First in sequence is **Method** (service). Its examples are *ftp://* and *http://.* Domain examples *axe ftp://netcom.com* and *ftp://ipswitch. com.* A file folder example is */pub.* A sub-folder example is */ne/netcom.* The file name examples are */WS_FTP.hlp, /wsftp.zip, /netiquette.html, ZftpO12.zip, java.net, java.sql, java.io.**. Password examples are say, dr_rajkamal@, id: 463754@, and 17: AXZ@.

In a hypertext document, an example of a URL for the ftp service is created by keying-in *<A HREF = "ftp:// ftp.mcom.com/ netscape/ window"> NetScape Windows </A>* . 'HREF' means a hypertext reference (link). The *ftp:// mcom.com/netscape/ window"*is the URL address from where the file can be downloaded. The URL is within the tags *<A >* . The link name 'NetScape Windows' is placed after that. Finally, </A> is the end of the link at that point. [Refer to Section 4.5.1 for details.]

TABLE 1.1

Service	*First*	*Second*	*Third*	*Fourth*	*Fifth*	*Sixth*
a	Method	domain				
a	Method	domain	file folder	file	name	
a	Method	domain	file folder	Subfolder/s)	filename	
b	Method	password	domain	file folder	sub-folder(s)	file name
b	Method	password	domain	file folder	file name	

Note : *a* : refers to an anonymous FTP. *b* : refers to non-anonymous FTP.

1. *Telnet Features*

Telnet is used for a session on a remote computer that follows logging-in to that system, (i) Consider a game on a remote server. The user plays the game there, (ii) Consider a university library computer with a catalogue. A catalogue is a specialized database of books. The user connects through a network, say, Internet, (iii) Consider initialization of a PERL program at the web site. The program processes the information put into a form by a client web browser. [The initialization is by the web site owner. The input is from the site user. The initialization may be for defining the authorizations and permissions to use and fill the form on the web.] How do we connect our computer with a remote computer for these uses? One method is to use FTP and transfer the data into our computer. Another method is by logging-in to the remote computer or remotely stored application itself and use that as it were on our terminal. The only difference is the use of the in-between connection (network). This network can nowadays be the Internet, and remote log-in can be made through the web browser using protocol-observing software called **Telnet.** A host computer program is called a Telnet server when it is the one that enables the **Telnet** client to enter into its system. A **Telnet client** is then a user program for logging-in to the server. The Telnet is also a part of the TCP/IP application suite. Using a remote computer system is a **Telnet session.** A Telnet client emulates the remote. It is a terminal emulation program. The **terminal emulation program** may also be for the VT 100 terminals. The client and server machines may differ in the formats for information interchange. For a Telnet session, the code translation is done not by the CPUs but by the terminal codes in the Telnet protocol itself.

Instead of Telnet, a terminal emulation program, TN3270 is used in an IBM 3270. It does not follow the Telnet protocol in the TCP/IP but connects and enables logging-in to this IBM mainframe.

A Telnet session was originally meant for UNIX machines. Nowadays, it is widely used on a Windows machine and through a web browser.

2. *Telnet Session and Programs*

We need one of the following for a Telnet session:

1. Web Browser for the Telnet

A remotely placed application is executed by using the web browser, for example NetScape Navigator. It links through a URL to a Telnet server. It can also be configured for an auto-start of Telnet client (software) for a session. [The Browsers does not provide the reverse. The results of the application are then displayed on the screen. The URL is defined by 'telnet://' for the method before the domain. A Telnet server may request a password. [If a server is open to all, the 'guest' or 'anonymous' or user e-mail address can be used instead of the password.] A Telnet client may include a general purpose communication program. The program is then used to (i) retrieve and save the incoming text, (ii) read by screen scrolling, (iii) to send information to other system, etc. For these, NetScape Navigator has a program. The Telnet client has the following general purpose communication programs: File, Edit, Options, Send, Browse, Window, and Help. These run by clicking on the corresponding buttons. The buttons are available on the top of the screen. Buttons for commands are available at the bottom of the screen. These include: 'Find' for searching; 'Search' to change files; 'Browse' to scan indexes; 'Connect' to use systems other than the system being used in the current Telnet session; and 'Bye' to quit the session.

2. UNIX Telnet

There can be a link from a Telnet server to our own using UNIX commands. A Telnet interface provides software for the UNIX Telnet. It then uses the UNIX commands. The interface is command 'telnet' in place of a command line, 'rlogin' for the remote logging-in. Once we login and after the password authorization a Telnet server uses Telnet commands. The 'get (filename)' command is to transfer files from the remote Telnet server. The 'put (filename)' can be used to transfer files to the remote host. The command 'quit' is for disconnecting from the remote server. We use the server now as if it were our terminal. The interface is, for example, a command line, a+rx reportingfile.pl. The a+ means that all users are permitted for the 'r' and 'x' features, using the PERL 'reporting file'.

3. Set of Files through the Telnet

A link can be made to a set of files for example, an application suite at the **Telnet server** on the Internet.

4. Telnet client Programs

There is no need to use the command lines-based interface. We can log in by using the Telnet client in place of the web browser. The Telnet client is not a part of Windows 98 but the latter has a general purpose communication program, HyperTerminal. We upgrade HyperTerminal for the Telnet sessions on Windows by downloading a Microsoft Telnet program. This can be downloaded from *http://www.hilgraeve.com/htpe.html*. It is a freeware. WinComm, QModem, and ProComm are WinSock compliant Telnet clients that have a general purpose communication program also. These give the features that upload and download the binary files between the Windows-based PC and the Telnet server. If we wish to connect for a Telnet session with a file library, we use XModem or ZModem or other communication programs.

3. *Telnet URLs*

A sequential URL address is in a sequence as shown in the successive columns. The first in sequence, Method is *telnet://*. The second in sequence is domain for the Telnet server.

1. Usenet Features

Let us first understand the importance of a bulletin board. In a college, there is a board called Notice Board or Bulletin Board where news is put up. The news may be about an annual function or cultural event or music festival. Teachers put news of seminars and other interesting articles on the board. The board is the college's bulletin (or notice) board. Similarly, there can be an electronic bulletin board of a group. A subscriber to a group could be living anywhere in the world. When do we need the Usenet service on the Internet? (i) Consider a group of computer students from a University.

They graduate and then join various organizations. Each one engages in a different profession. How can they keep in touch? The news of interest to them is marriage, job changeover, new e-mail addresses, new achievements, etc. (ii) Consider a business group who would like to announce a new product for distributors and users of that product. How can the group distribute this news to them? (iii) Consider a hobby group on roses who would like to post news of a new variety genetically engineered by a member and which is in full bloom. How can the group of hobbyists on roses get this news? (iv) Consider a railway company interested in distributing news of each train. Its route, time of departure, time of arrival at the destination, reservation position at each hour would be of interest to many. How can it be done? How do we get the news through the Internet? A Newsgroup for each of these groups can be posted on the electronic bulletin board available on the Internet. Each board has a collection of news items on a topic, or will have news posted by a member of a forum or group.

The Usenet is a service for accessing a globally distributed bulletin board. Usenet is the name of the Internet service that provides a means for access by a particular Newsgroup of specific information of different kinds.

Usenet provides only the text messages. About 10% of Internet uses are by the Usenet and other Newsgroups. It is more than the e-mail (~ 7.5%). It is however less than the FTP (~ 15%) and the web use (~ 40%). We must also observe Netiquette for posting the news to any Newsgroup. Netiquette means an accepted behaviour on the network during writing an article. There is a welcome greeting at the start. Never put false news on an Internet message, especially, death or accident unless confirmed. Be kind to other's articles. Never key-in flaming news. Draft your replies coolly before sending. Read coolly before a reply or discussion.

2. Difference between Multi-list e-mails and Newsgroups

What are the differences between a news posted by a Newsgroup and an e-mail to a large number of e-mail addresses from a list? (i) First, Newsgroup messages are for the group not individuals as in the e-mails. The messages are not permanently stored in an account on the server that is somewhere on the Internet. We first download the header of each message. When we find a message appropriate then we download the entire message. We can save it also. (ii) We can subscribe to a Newsgroup. We run the Subscribe utility to join a Newsgroup. We can read news by a Newsreader program. (iii) The protocol is not according to the e-mail protocols PoP3 or SMTP or ESMTP. The protocol is either UUCP or NNTP. (iv) Newsgroup utility supports text only. [A few recent ones additionally feature multimedia through the URLs and MIME supports.] (v) All ISPs now support e-mails. Newsgroup support, however, may not be available, as there has to be a separate Newsgroup server which follows the protocol other than that of the **TCP/IP** suite.

3. *Usenet Hosts*

There are thousands of hosts to backup the Newsgroups on the Usenet service. It is a powerful utility for events, news, technical articles, sports-news, news-readers' opinions and reactions. The ISPs also provide Usenet servers just as they do the web servers. Each Usenet host has a database of the articles that are up-to date, and exchanges these with other Usenet hosts.

4. *Types of Usenet groups*

1. Un-moderated Usenet

A huge collection of groups or topics on the Usenet is said to be un-moderated. Any news for the group is directly posted to the Usenet. There is no one to filter and make judgements on the appropriateness of the messages. Any one can post the news.

2. Moderated Usenet

A huge collection of groups or topics on the Usenet can be moderated by a person. The messages that are posted are first directed automatically to a moderator. The moderator examines, filters, edits and finally puts the result on the Usenet.

5. *Major Newsgroups*

Usenet Newsgroups are as follows, (i) 'sci' for science topics, (ii) 'soc' for social topics, (iii) 'comp' for computer topics, (iv) 'rec' for recreation topics, (v) 'talk' for posting opinion on different topics, (vi) 'misc' for miscellaneous subjects, like job search, tax, health, education, etc., (vii) 'news' for the news from Newsreader Software, Network News, etc. Other Newsgroups are 'bionet' for biology, 'alt' for the alternative topics, and 'biz' for business topics, etc. Besides the USENET, there can be the **Private News** servers in an organization. There may also be additional multimedia supports.

6. *Usenet Protocols*

1. UUCP for UNIX Usenet

The word Usenet was coined by a group of Unix machine users. It is a short form of user network. The protocol used was called Unix to Unix Copy Protocol **(UUCP).** The earlier News-software, made by *Steve Bellovin*, has now been upgraded. The upgrade has been made for not only the Unix network but also for the Internet. UUCP is however not a part of the TCP/IP. ISPs support it due to its popularity.

2. NNTPAn General Usenet Protocol

Nowadays the news-reader program used is the Net News Transport Protocol **(NNTP).** There is a unique ID (identity) number assigned to each news or article. This helps in filtering the news so that a user does not receive the same message twice.

3. NINTH with AdditionalSSLs

NINTH supports the creation as well as maintenance of private Newsgroups at big sites. Communication is secure and free from unnecessary violation as there are facilities for encryption, server authentication, and message integrity. This additional security has been provided through a layer called Secure Socket Layer (SSL).

7. *Usenet Programs*

A popular application software for Newsgroups is a client program called NetScape Collabra. To join a Newsgroup, we have to first run the subscribe utility. We can locate an appropriate Newsgroup by using Collabra. This can be done by keying in the full name of the Newsgroup, or if we are not sure of the full name, by keying in a few characters from the name. We may also search for a group by a keyword. When the appropriate Newsgroup has been selected, click O.K. to join in.

We can interact with Newsgroups in many ways. We can switch to a new server or to another subscribed Newsgroup,. When we post a news (article) we can specify that our message (article) be excluded from the indexes. This is in case we post to a subscribed private Newsgroup. If we wish our article to be included in the indexes, we can also specify a list of keywords that may be mentioned in the header for the indexes. This is in case we post to or subscribe to a public Newsgroup. The Collabra also has a utility called 'Newsreader'. It is for fetching the news.

Outlook Express News is another popular application software. It is also accessed by thousands of Newsgroups. Using Outlook Express News we can configure the 'Newsreader', connect to a New Server, subscribe, view, download, and read articles off-line. We can use news filters. We can create new messages. We can reply to a Newsgroup message. We can also reply privately to an author by e-mail.

We can also search for a Newsgroup worth subscribing to using sites like AltaVista and Yahoo.

There is a freeware for the Newsgroup service. It can be downloaded from *http:// www.forteinc. com/agent/*

8. *Web Browser for the Usenet*

A remotely placed Newsgroup message can be located using the web browser. It can be accessed through a link in a URL. The results of the application display on the screen through the Browser browsing. The URL is defined by 'news:'

for the method, Usenet, and an ID name or number after that. NetScape Navigator and Internet Explorer have the Web Browsers that includes 'NewsReader' utility. The advanced features are as follows :

1. *Text can be read off-line or on-line:* On-line reading reduces charges and can be used when the connection charges are paid as a flat rate on a monthly or yearly basis. If charges are to be paid per hour, it is more economical to work off-line.
2. *Article Alerts and Watch Lists:* Let us assume that there is some important News that we have not read because we are not connected to the Internet. The alert program, which runs in background in the Newsreader program gives an audio tone or a visual alert, to inform the user that there is some news to be read. The Watch List program reads News or articles defined in the Watchlist automatically.
3. *The sorting support:* This program sorts the News author-wise, date-wise, file size-wise, etc.
4. *Search:* We can search for Newsgroup articles using keywords and/or by subject.
5. *URL Support:* A specific News with an identity can be obtained by a URL in a hypertext document. It brings a web user to the News. There may be the clickable URLs in an article. This is a sophisticated feature in certain Newsreader programs. The receiver of the article can click to a selected document. The document can be found in the pages that the URL points to. The clickable URLs are usually sent as attachments to a message. A sequential URL address is in a sequence that has been shown in successive columns
6. *Content Sensitive Help:* While reading a document, help may be needed to understand the contents. A content sensitive help provides that.
7. *Duplicate Files Handling:* This feature discards duplicate files.
8. *Cross Post-Management:* There can be a cross post-management. This means that a message that has

been read by one member of newsgroup initiates sufficient action and therefore it appears as if all the subscribers have read the message. For example, an appeal for some help may elicit a response from only a few members but that alone is sufficient for the purpose.

9. *Threading:* Threading groups together associated subjects, so that they can be conveniently read or downloaded. For example, we can group together the 'comp' Newsgroup and sports articles.
10. *Read/Write News-record File:* There can be a file to keep a record of the read/write articles. This helps when we use the Newsreader program at different locations.
11. *Filters:* We may like to specify certain criteria to identify articles that are interesting but have not yet been read. The messages that satisfy that criteria filter in and the rest are discarded. For example, we may specify key words. If the subject for News has words that are among those key words, then the mail niters in. We can define criteria for filtering that is based on the logical terms And, Or or Not.
12. *Lock:* We can lock or unlock an article to prevent or allow public access.
13. *Copy Self:* This helps in case when an article is created on-line. It allows the sender to save copy in his own file.
14. *Courtesy Copy:* This allows us to specify an address to which a copy of an article created online must be forwarded.
15. *File Extension Translation:* The extensions of four letters can be converted to extensions of three letters and *vice versa*. For example, 'html' to 'htm'.
16. *Folders:* Different articles can be saved into different folders. For example, the articles from Newsgroups, 'comp' and 'soc' can be saved in different folders.
17. *Frames:* Different frames in the articles show up in the special frames on the screen. This gives ease of reading. Images can also scale into the frames.

18. *MIME (Multipurpose Internet Mail Extension) Support:* An extension is the first packet in interchange message. A program identifies the file as being of a certain extension type. MIME is in RFC 1341 standard. MIME attachments allow the user to encode or decode binary attachments in the articles, for example jpg files.
19. *Multimedia Support:* Usenet is text-based. However, in a private Newsgroup, there can be multimedia support whenever MIME Support is available.
20. *Messaging (and) Application Programs Interface (MAPI):* This feature helps the sender to create a message in a special way. During keying in the message, a MAPI compliant file can be selected.
21. *Purging:* This feature helps in hiding or discarding the Old News, or select Newsgroup articles. There may be a Trash Box feature. A Trash Box is where all the discarded News can be stored automatically, and they remain there till completely removed.
22. *Kill List:* There is automatically ignores articles on a particular subject or from a particular Newsgroup.
23. *Multiple Signatures:* We may like to append different types of signatures for different Newsgroups. The signature can be *automatically appended* at the end of an every out News to a Newsgroup. The signature may be the sender's name, sender's Newsgroup, designation, company, phone number, fax number or e-mail address, URL for sender's web page, etc.
24. *Multiple Windows:* This feature helps in creating multiple windows for different articles or Newsgroups. This makes discussion of a subject more effective and helps in forwarding messages to other Newsgroups.
25. *Address Book:* This is a master e-mail mailing list or contact information for all members of the Newsgroup. When we recall this address book, it helps in selecting addresses where the message ought to be sent.

26. *Agent:* An **agent** is a utility that works automatically as programmed even if we exit the application. Examples are as follows. An agent provides a **check for new News** at a Newsgroup. An agent deletes temporary files. An agent may send **automatically generated messages** to the Newsgroup; for example, New Year greetings. The agents can be *scheduled* to activate on a particular day and time.
27. *Drag and Drop:* We can drag an object or file and drop it into the article created for the Newsgroup.
28. *Select Specific Author by Flat Mode Support:* A specific author may belong to a different Newsgroup. [For example, an author puts an article to a Newsgroup and also puts another article at another Newsgroup.] We can select the specific author articles by flat mode support. Flat mode support means a support independent of the specific Newsgroup.
29. *Spell Check:* Checking the spelling is essential before an article is ready. Even correction to a reply message that copies a part of text from the original mail may also be programmable.
30. *Quote Support:* It permits an author to paste or append quotations from other articles. This helps in understanding the context of the article.
31. *SSL Support:* This supports encryption, authentication, and message integrity by the addition to the NINTH through a protocol Secure Socket Layer (SSL).
32. *E-mail Support:* This supports e-mail to a group member in a Newsgroup.
33. *Stitching Support:* This supports the orderly placing of the binary attachments, even if sent separately.
34. *Tags Support:* This support places the tags for the News for ease of viewing.
35. *Themes Feature:* The user creates theme-specific buttons to connect easily to articles on specific themes.

'GOPHER', 'WAIS', 'ARCHIE' AND 'VERONICA'

1. Gopher Features

A gopher means a rodent. The University of Minnesota created a tool for information-gathering and developed a **Gopher client and a Gopher+.** A Gopher client is a user program for logging-in to the files located on the **Gopher servers.** Gopher+ has the extended information and interactive forms. A gopher client displays a list of menu options in the running text. Like a link in the web page, a menu can take us to a new menu or to a document or data base. Key searches are possible in remote databases on Gopher servers. Then there are the **Ask** Forms. Ask forms contain text, an item to select from among several answers as well as spaces for filling-in the answers. An Ask form helps a **Gopher administrator** to support the enrolment, registration, examination, tests, and advanced query language features. A Gopher administrator is one authorized to process the Ask Forms and configure a Gopher server.

All the Gopher servers interconnect on the Internet They are similar to FTP servers and yet different. Instead of a filename, we use the contents of the file for the read, save or search from a Gopher server. A Gopher server is one that hosts the directories and files that are retrievable by the Gopher Clients and Gopher+.

Gopher servers store large amounts of information like a web server. However, Web servers have now greatly overtaken the Gopher servers.

The Gopher protocol is also a part of TCP/IP application suite like an FTP or Telnet. Gopher uses TCP in the transport layer. The Gopher session was originally meant for UNIX machines. Nowadays, it is used through a web browser. Gopher documents can be read like a web page and can be scrolled. There are bookmarks instead of the URLs in a gopher document.

2. The Programs

We need one of the followings for a Gopher session:

1. **Web Browser for the Gopher:** A remotely placed

application executes by using a webbrowser; for example, NetScape Navigator. It links through a URL to a Gopher server. It can also configure to auto-start a Gopher client (software) to conduct a search in the Gopher space.

2. **Gopher clients:** Originally, a Gopher client and a Gopher+ were the UNIX commands. Now a Windows-based Gopher client program is WSGopher32. **Jughead** is a Gopher search engine.

3. Internet Chat

1. *An Internet Relay Chat Features*

An e-mail response may come the same day or not at all. It all depends on the receiver. A Newsgroup article posted by a member may not elicit discussion or response from the other members. Can we interchange messages among the group members on-line? Can we chat through the Internet as if we are having a conference? How does one play chess on-line with a partner or with several partners at the same time? **Internet Relay Chat** (IRC) is a worldwide network for the real time text conversations. The conversations are held by keying-in text by each participating member. A chat can be between two or more members. The chats are on a channel or a chat room. A channel means a theme or topic. A chat room is also a chat channel. Each channel or a chat room has a specific name. There are special IRC servers. Yahoo provides a popular chat server. Most IRC servers are on the networks of EFFNET, Undernet and DALnet. These connect to the several IRC clients in real time.

What are the differences between a chat using the IRC and news postings in a Newsgroup? (i) First, the messages are to group members who are on line and not off-line. All participating members who are active during a chat session get each message. All are on the Internet at the same time, (ii) The messages are not permanently stored at any client, (iii) We can join a chat session. We run the 'join channel' utility to join a Chat group. We can chat using a Chat program, **MIRC.** (iv) We can use the short abbreviations for conversation and use shortcuts to communicate emotions, (v) The protocol **(IRC protocol)**, is different and there are special **IRC servers.**

2. *Web-based, point-to-point and Telnet-based Chats*

A web browser has chat features through the third party plug-ins. A **plug-in** is an additional software or utility added in a program. Third party means that software is from another source that of the Browser. A common interest group can meet at a common web page on a site. A common interest group can develop a web site by talking on Chat.

The Chat program can permit users to communicate directly. Both have the e-mail addresses. Certain chat programs support IRC protocol also.

Telnet permits remote logins. The hosts can include a real time chat program through the Telnet

3. *MUDs*

The MUDs are the Multi-User Dungeons. A Dungeon manipulates, through text commands, a fantasy in three dimensions through graphical user interface. A chat system is then used for an association playing a game. There can be support to a voice channel.

4. *Other Chat Programs*

There are programs that may not need IRC servers and may use IRC protocol. One is **PowWow.** Other is **People Connection.** It is on AOL (America On Line, an ISP in USA). **'People Connection'** has an application 'Find a Chat'. Other applications are Private Chat, Members Chat, Featured Chat, Channel Chat.

5. *Chat Commands*

1. /JOIN #'channel name'. It is used for joining a channel. A welcome message may also be displayed on accepting a request to join.

2. /QUIT. It is for disconnecting and quitting the channel. '/QUIT Bye!' is for communicating the message bye! , then quit.
3. /CLEAR. It is for clearing the screen.
4. /LIST. It is for listing the number of participants in the channel. /LIST #topic will retrieve a list of participants on a topic. /LIST MAX 16 retrieves a list in which there are a maximum of 16 members./LIST MIN25 retrieves a list in which there are a minimum of 25 members.
5. /INVITE 'nameO4' 'topic'. It is used for inviting a member named 'nameO4' to join a 'topic'. Default is current channel (topic).
6. /IGNORE nameO2. It is for suppressing a message to nameO2 on the participating channel. /IGNORE s*. It is for suppressing a message to members with nicknames starting with s on the participating channel. The wildcard * can be placed at the end after a few characters or before any of the characters. Users have the right to insist on select criteria to restrict members not having the same qualifications or quality. Members not having the listed criteria are ignored.
7. /KICK 'nameO5'. A channel operator can kick a user off the channel in case of misconduct or if the user refuses to follow net user-ethics (Chatiquette). Chatiquette is **Netiquette** during a Chat. That means an accepted behaviour on the network during the chat. Reciprocate greetings. Be kind to other views and emotions. Never key-in an offensive or flaming message.
8. /TOPIC #topic01. This is for changing the discussion topic from one to another. It informs all the participating members of the change.
9. /MSG nameO6. This is used to inform user nameO6 that there is a private message and to post a message that the user is busy to attend to that private message.

10. /QUERY nameO6. It is to inform user nameOG that there is a window for the query and that the query can be put there till the user is free to attendto it.
11. /WHOIS name07. Let 'nameO7' is the nickname. This command is to find about the details of user nicknamed 'name07'.
12. /NOTIFY nameO9. It is to send alerts to a new user nameO9.
13. /AWAY 'on vacations' to convey a message 'on vacations' to the other participants whenever the others invite a participant.

6. *Internet Relay Chat (IRC) Features*

1. **Direct point-to-point support:** A Chat program can permit direct client-to-client (DCC) support without using the IRC servers. Both communicate directly on-line through the e-mail addresses.
2. **Address Book:** A Chat address list helps in selecting whom to join in the channel.
3. **Yellow Pages:** These are the important addresses in a list in the Chat program. Chat sites can be quickly searched to locate a group that is of interest.
4. **URL Support:** A specific web page is obtained by clicking on a URL in a hypertext document. The clickable URLs are the attachments to a conversation.
5. **Chat Schedule:** This helps to switch to the web browser and connect to a scheduled page for a Chat. A third party plug-in may be needed by the Web Browser.
6. **Multi Frames or Split Screen Support:** There can be different frames for conversations between different participants. This gives ease of reading and images can also scale into the frames.
7. **Channel Filtering:** This allows us to conduct a search using key words. The channels that result in a match can filter in. We can specify the channels or topics to be filtered in. We can define criteria for filtering using the logical terms And, Or, and Not.

8. **Aliases or Nicknaming:** We may store the abbreviations of the standard replies or names of the participating members. An alias or nickname can automatically be expanded to the full standard reply or name. For example, P.8 for P. Balasubramanian or Deep for Deep and Deep. For example, Scientist, for a participating member knowing much about science.
9. **Macros, New Buttons and Hot Keys Support:** These saves time on the Internet. These are converted by the chat program from their short forms, (i) We can define a macro for a reply. We can convey an emotion, say, laughing by the macro. For example, BTW is for 'by the way'. AFK is for 'away from keyboard'. For a cat, >^,,^<. For the heart <3.:::: It gives smile:::: for a scene in a drama or play. (ii) We can also add a screen Button instead of a macro. For example, {{{{Darling}}}} for expressing love during a Chat with the spouse! We simply click on the button when starting a Chat, (iii) We can also define a hot key or a combination of keys instead of a macro. For example, define F6 key as a hot key for a laughing or define F10 for a sad expression.
10. **Multi Sessions Support:** there can be different sessions for conversations between multiple participants. We may switch between the various sessions.
11. **Colored and Styled Text Support:** This is a support for the coloring the text and setting the text styles.
12. **User Identity Support:** A client-to-client protocol (CTCP) is used for the IRC server and IRC client. This is for finding the real name, e-mail address, phone number, address of a Chat channel member. A personal curriculum vitae can also be stored on the IRC server. This is then recalled by a **Personal Biography support** in the program.
13. **Event Handlers:** It is a utility to convey the joining or quitting of a member.
14. **Drag and Drop:** We can drag an object or image

from a file. We then drop it into the conversation during a chat.

15. **Quote Support:** It permits the user to paste or append quotations from an object. This helps in making conversation lively.
16. **Sound Support:** Some Chat programs may have sounds or voice to make conversations lively.

QUESTIONS

1. List the protocols and their use at the application layer in the Internet.
2. What do we mean by ISP, Backbone Service Provider and Network Access Point operator?
3. Define World Wide Web.
4. What are the following personalities famous for? (a) Bill Gates, (b) Vinton Cerf. (c) Robert Metcalfe. (d) Tim Bernes Lee. (e) Marc Andreesen.
5. What are the services available on the Internet?
6. What are the bit rates with interconnections as Tl, T3, DS3, OC-3C, OC-12 and OC-48?
7. Differentiate between http, https, ftp, telnet and usenet services.
8. Describe the features in HTTP 1.1.
9. What are the different types of headers in an HTTP message from a client?
10. What are the different types of headers in an HTTP message from a server?
11. How does a user connect to the Internet?
12. What should be the features one looks for while selecting an ISP?
13. What is a portal? Connect to the Internet and surf through a portal. List the features of that portal.
14. How many bytes are there in an IP address in IPv4?
15. Each byte is separated by a dot when an IP address is used in a software? Why?
16. Why do we use a domain name instead of an IP address?
17. How does the domain name convert to an IP address?
18. What do we mean by com and .edu?
19. What do we mean by a MAC address?
20. How does a MAC address convert to an IP address? How does an IP address convert to a MAC address? When do we need these conversions?
21. Why does a routing algorithm generate a dynamic IP address?

22. What do we mean by DNS? What is a DNS server?
23. What is a URL? How does a URL differ from the domain name?
24. Use tracert utility on Windows for finding the IP addresses for each router and thus the hops for the packets. Run the utility tracert for web sites of interest. Why does this utility give the same last IP address but different in-between addresses in different runs? Now prepare a table of 10 rows for the IP addresses and their respective domain names.
25. Explain the terms, host, resource, path and port.
26. What is the significance of sign '@' in an e-mail address?
27. Explain the terms, WinSock, Socket, UDP header and Dialup PPP account.
28. List features of an e-mail program.
29. What is MAPI?
30. Explain the terms, JPEG and jpg file, MPEG and mpg file and gif.
31. Describe MIME types and MIME attachment.
32. Describe POP3?
33. Describe SMTP?
34. Describe the meaning of 'Hypertext'. What is a web browser?
35. What do we mean by a sequential search and nonlinear search for a resource at a website?
36. What is WAP?
37. How does a cellular phone browse through the Web?
38. List the seven OSI layers for WAP?
39. What do we mean by 'Protocol tunneling'?
40. What are the differences between an anonymous FTP and non-anonymous FTP?
41. What are the advantages and disadvantages in TFTP with respect to FTP?
42. What do we mean by a virtual terminal? How does the TELNET provide the virtual terminal?
43. How does a Telnet session initiate?
44. What do we mean by a Gopher server?
45. Describe the advanced features of the Usenet service?

46. What is NNTP?
47. What do we mean by a bulletin board?
48. What are MUDs?
49. What are the features of Internet Relay Chat?
50. What do we mean by VoIP?

Internet Servics

1. OBJECTIVES

- Understanding the overview of internet technology
- Different types of internet connectivity
- Describe various types of Web resources
- Different types Browsers, search engines
- Identify the different types of Internet Tools

2. PREAMBLE

The internet offers a number of services to its user. Many types of Internet services are available. The following are among the most popular and useful:

They are

- E-Mail—Electronic Mail
- FTP—File Transfer Protocol
- Usenet News
- Telnet—Remote login feature
- WWW overview

3. E_MAIL—ELECTRONIC MAIL

EMail allows sending of information from one computer to another. In other words it allows transmission of text in machine-readable form one computer to another. The different elements of Email are :

- the address of the both recipient/sender,
- a subject line, and
- the message

1. Email addresses:

E-mail address contains two parts. They are USERID, DOMAIN. The domain can be classified in two types. They are Organizational domain and Geographic domain. The USERID and DOMAIN is separated by '@' symbol. For example, the Email address of MIT and Anna University library are:

e.g.: 1. siemit@giasmd01.vsnl.net.in
2. annalib@sirnetm.ernet.in

4. WHAT IS FTP?

FTP, File transfer Organiza, connects to remote sites and to exchange data between two computers. The FTP allows computer users to download files and store these files on their own hard disk. The files may be any type of data, i e. programs, text, graphis, photographs. It also allows limited directory-related operations on that site.

5. TELENET

Telenet connects to remote computer locations as if you are a terminal for that location. Using Telnet one must know the name of the host i.e. Either domain name or IP address and login name. For example, if any one needs details about INFORMATION ON TECHNOLOGY the domain name and login name is

e.g. telnet debra.dgbt.doc.ca login name: chat

Similarly to connect libraries the domain name and login name is

e.g. telnet nessie.cc.wwu.edu
login name: libs

6. USENET NEWS

It is the bulletin board service of Internet. It is read and contributed to on a daily basis. Vast amount of communication and interaction can take place over a short period. Mainly it is used for propagation of news.

There are different News group, organized according to topic. They are

alt.	alternative topics
clair.	Businesses, products
comp.	computer
talk.	Talk and discussion
rec.	recreation

7. NETWORK NAVIGATION TOOLS

The different internet navigational tools are :

- Archie
- Gopher
- Veronica
- Jughead
- WWW—World Wide Web
- WAIS—Wide Area Information Server

1. ARCHIE

Archie is a program that maintains a list of available files at FTP sites around the internet. The contents of information are :

— Filename
— Filesize
— Type of file

— File description

2. GOPHER

It is really guide on the internet. Developed in University of Minnesota. It allows to access databases from all around the internet through menu structure. As name implies it will "go for" the data or topic that is specified. Gopher server can be accessed by typing ID.

e.g. Gopher .msu.edu
[M.S University, India]

3. VERONICA

Very Easy Rodent Oriented Netwi6de Index to Computerised Archive (VERONICA) is used as a tool in conjunction with gopher. The folks at the University of Nevada develop it. It is basically an extension to gopher.

4. JUGHEAD

It is another add-on service for gopher. It is very similar to Veronica but narrow your search

8. WORLD WIDE WEB

It is wide area hypermedia information retrieval initiative aiming to give universal access to a large universe of documents. The idea was explored in 1960\s. but began to use began in 1989.

The web started as a small hypertext-based network of documents, where the document is distributed over several machines on the internet. At present, the web is truly world wide with web documents literally spanning the globe.

9. INFORMATION SERVICES

The other information services that can be used in internet are:

- Electronic Discussion Lists and Forums
- Electronic journals

- Library catalogues
- Universities
- Computer Wide Information Systems (CWIS).
- Database Access on Internet
- Data and Software Archives
- Companies and organization
- Multiuser Dimensional Games (MUDS)

10. CONCLUSION

The use of Internet provides a much enhanced interface between the user and the information. By use of fixed or moving images, combined with text and voice, information can be provided in forms which are more easily interpretable by the recipient. Some of the applications listed above may appear frivolous but the impact on many aspects of business and social life will be significant.

QUESTIONS

1. What is e-mail?
2. What is FTP?
3. Discuss in detail about TELENET.
4. Explain the Network Navigation Tools.
5. Describe the World Wide Web.
6. Discuss the Information Services.

3

Net Information Sources—Evaluation

1. OBJECTIVES

- Understanding the need for the evaluation of web resources
- Analysing Different types of information sources
- Describe need for initial appraisal
- Different Evaluation Criteria
- Find out the challenges in the web resources
- Identify the means of evaluating the web pages

2. INTRODUCTION

There are enormous growths in websites, including academic websites. Most of the academic websites are static in nature. The updation of information and proper maintenance is the basic requirement of any web site. The users' satisfaction, on the website is most incredible one which can be termed as Web Credibility. Unfortunately the functionality, design, quality of information, etc. are not properly adopted by the websites, according to the web credibility standards. Various researchers have conducted studies on Web Credibility to understand the different factors of users' expectation in websites. Commercial websites are dynamic in nature and will adopt the changes of the user expectations quickly. But service industries like academic institutions will take more time to react.

3. NEED FOR THE EVALUATION OF WEB RESOURCES

- Web resources are self-publishing medium
- Not all sources are equally valuable/reliable
- Sometimes, may not be authentic/accurate
- May not be current
- May not be filtered/mediated
- No standard in the publication

4. ANALYSING INFORMATION SOURCES

- Initial Appraisal
- Content Appraisal

1. Initial Appraisal

- Author
- Date of Publication
- Edition/Revision
- Publisher
- Title
- Contributors/Collaborators

2. Content Analysis

- Intended audience
- Objective reasoning
- Coverage
- Writing/Presentation Style
- Evaluative reviews

5. CATEGORY OF WEBSITES

- Advocacy websites
- Business/Marketing WebPages
- News WebPages
- Informational WebPages
- Personal WebPages

6. EVALUATION CRITERIA

- Accuracy
- Authority
- Accessibilitv
- Arrangement
- Currency
- Coverage
- Completeness
- Objectivity
- Response time
- Stability
- Style
- Target Audience

1. Accuracy

- Is the information reliable and error-free?
- Are there editors and fact checkers?
  - # Currently no Web standards exist to ensure accuracy
  - # Not fully developed
  - # Almost any one can publish on the Web
  - # Editors and/or fact checkers do not verify many Web resources

2. Authority

- Is it clearly stated, who is the author?
- What is author's position, qualifications, past writings etc?
- Is the Author associated with an organisation?

- What are the basic goals and objectives of the organisation?
- How reputable is the publisher?
- Who is the sponsor? Is reputable?
- Is there any contact address, phone, fax, e-mail address?
  - # Often difficult to determine authorship of Web Resources
  - # Publisher responsibility often not shown
  - # If author's name is listed, qualifications are frequently absent.

3. Accessibility

- How easy it is to get to the site?
- Can it be read by many kinds of software?
- Do they prefer a particular browser?
- How easy it is to use the site?
  - # Some of the e-journals are in PDF format that require Acrobat Reader.
  - # Mention to be made, if needed, about the name of the Software to access the page.

4. Arrangement

- Should be logical
- Easy to use
- Links/Buttons of the Web Page should be consistent
- Screens should be easy to be read

5. Currency

- Is the content of the work up-to-date?
- Is the publication date clearly indicated?
- Whether the Page is dated?
- When it is last updated?
- How current the links áre'?
- Whether any/some of the links expired? Or Moved?
- What is the frequency of updation?

- Are there any other indications that the material is kept current?
  - # Dates not always included on WebPages
  - # If included, a date may have various meanings, such as
- Date first created
- Date placed on the Web
- Date last revised.

6. Coverage

- What topics are included in the work?
- To what depth are topics explored?
- What languages are covered?
- What time period is covered?
  - # Web coverage may differ from print or other media coverage.
  - # Often difficult to determine the extent of the Web coverage.

7. Completeness

- Information provided should be complete.

8. Objectivity

- Is the information presented with a minimum bias?
- To what extent is the information trying to sway the opinion of the audience?
  - # Web often function as a virtual Soapbox.
  - # Goals/aims of persons or groups presenting material often not clearly stated.

9. Response Time

- How much time it takes to load a Web Page?
  - # Depends on the client server's efficiency

10. Stability

- Is the site stable?
- Does the link address change frequently?
- If the address changes, whether the old page is left open with new link or address?

11. Style

- Are the sentences and directions clear?
- Is the grammar correct?
- Is it interactive, so that user can use buttons, forms and feedback instruments?

12. Target Audience

- In each and every source the targeted audience should be defined.
  # Relevancy varies with purpose and user's needs

7. ADDITIONAL CHALLENGES PRESENTED BY WEB RESOURCES

- Use of Hypertext links
- Use of Frames
- Search Engines can retrieve pages out of context or noise or overload of information
- Marketing-oriented Web Pages
- Blending of entertainment, information and advertising
- Software requirement may limit access
- Instability of Web Pages
- Susceptibility of Web Pages to alteration
- Quality of Web Pages linked to original Web Page may vary.

8. WEB PAGE EVALUATION PROCEDURE

Step 1 : Identify the type of Page

Step 2 : Use appropriate checklist

Step 3 : Based on the checklist criteria, determine relative quality of page.

9. CONCLUSION

- Web Evaluation techniques are only in the beginning and need to be developed further.
- Technology is outpacing the ability to create/develop standards and guidelines.
- Establishing evaluation procedures will be an ongoing evolutionary process.

QUESTIONS

1. Explain the need for the evaluation of Web Resources
2. Write briefly on Content Analysis
3. List out the Various Categories of Web sites
4. Discuss some Additional Challenges presented by Web Resources
5. Describe the Web Page Evaluation Procedure

PART II

Web Resources

World Wide Web

1. OBJECTIVES

After studying this lesson, you should be able to:

- Understanding the overview of internet technology
- Different types of internet connectivity
- Describe various types of Web resources
- Different types Browsers, search engines
- Identify the different types of Internet Tools

2. INTRODUCTION

The WWW is defined as a "wide area hypermedia information retrieval tool aiming to give universal access to a large universe of documents". It has afforded the users of computer networks with a consistent means to access variety of media in a simplified fashion. World Wide Web is referred to as 'WWW', W3 or simply.

'The WEB". The WWW is a vast collection of text, images and video data scattered across networks and computers around the world.

According to Tim Berners-lee, one of the Web's chief architects from CERN, The World Wide Web is "the universe of network accessible information, an embodiment of human knowledge. It has a body of software, a set of protocols and conventions. WWW used hypertext and multimedia techniques to make the web easy for anyone to roam, browse and contribute to."

What is World Wide Web?

- It is one part of the internet
- Uses 'Hyperlinks' to link information dynamically and interactively
- Can use text, Graphics, Sound and Video
- Each Document on the web has a unique URL (Like an Address)
- Pages are written in Hyper Text Markup Language (HTML)

3. WWW AND INTERNET

The WWW is used in the Internet and is part of it. WWW refers to a body of information while the Internet refers to the physical side of global network. It used the internet to transmit hypermedia documents between computer users internationally. It is a navigational tool on the Internet that enables browsing information linked to other related information. WWW also uses a set of protocols and conversions. It is built around a set of shared rules for communicating data requests across a network and for responding to those requests.

4. RESOURCES ON THE WEB

Web resources are identified with a special name called "Uniform Resource Identifiers (URIS)". These identify objects that may be accessed on the Web. Web pages are identified through its "Uniform Resource Locators (URLs). URLs are simply, address for documents on the Web. The different parts of the URL are:

- Protocol (Eg. *http*—Hyper Text Transfer Protocol)
- Hostname
- Filename.

The syntax will be ***Protocol::llhostnamelfilename***

Eg. (i) http: / /www.drtc.edu
(ii) http: / /www.microsoft.com

The URL describes the protocol used to reach the target server, the host system on which the document resides, the directory path to the document, and the document file name. The uniform naming scheme for resources is makes the World Wide Web such a rich information environment.

5. WEB MODEL

The Web components are:

WEB Server—for storing the information
WEB Browsers—for retrieving the information

1. WEB Server

In order to deliver the information, it is to be stored in a particular machine. This machine is called WEB server. In other words, it is a particular machine on the network, running software necessary to recognize and accommodate web requests. The storage and retrieval part is handled by web server. The three basic tasks of the web server are:

Listening for request, Interpreting the valid request, Providing those resources.

2. WEB Browser

Web browser, also called a "browser", to access content published on a web server. Web browsers are software programs that allow accessing the graphical portion of the Internet. Browsers allow the users to access various web sites and view the web pages. They provide the option of entering the URL of the site to be visited. Browser software can be divided into the following two categories:

- Text-based browsers—Lynx
- GUI-based browsers—NCSA Mosaic, Netscape Navigator, Internet Explore, etc.

CONCLUSION

Internet is the largest storehouse of information. It is the only place in the world where one can fine information in such large amounts on a variety of subjects.

QUESTIONS

1. What is World Wide Web?
2. Elaborately discuss WWW and Internet.
3. Discuss some of the resources available on the web.
4. Explain in detail about the web model.

5

Web Portal

1. OBJECTIVES

- Understanding the overview of internet technology
- Different types of internet connectivity
- Describe various types of Web resources
- Different types Browsers, search engines
- Identify the different types of Internet Tools

2. INTRODUCTION

It is commonly referred to as simply a portal, a Web site or service that offers a broad array of resources and services, such as e-mail, forums, search engines, and on-line repositories. Traditionally, a portal denotes a gate, a door, or entrance. In the context of the World Wide Web, it is the next logical step in the evolution to a digital culture. Web pages are not completely self-referential anymore, but allow for personalization, workflow, notification, knowledge management and groupware, infrastructure functionality, and integration of information and applications. The idea of a portal is to collect information from different sources and create a single point of access to information a library of categorized and personalized content. It is very much the idea of a personalized filter into the web. Portals are often the first page the web browser loads when users get connected to the Web or that users tend to visit as an anchor site. But now most of the traditional search engines and web sites have transformed themselves into Web portals to attract and keep a larger audience. A web portal is a collection of all pages under one domain. For example, www.msuniversity.com, the online portal for collection and dissemination of information resources. So this is our web portal. No matter how small or large your institute is, members can profit enormously from a web portal.

The reduced publishing costs alone are worth establishing a web portal for your institute. Imagine your all member institutes resources being collected and organized in such a way that any member can get up to date information from it. It may be documents, pictures, videos, lecture notes, exam results, live class room videos, etc. Whenever you offer a new course or organizing program, you simply update your web portal any time of day and it will reach the members as early as possible. A web portal is a special website designed to act as a gateway to give convenient access to users.

3. WHAT A WEB PORTAL DOES?

- Enables universal login
- Handles both structured and unstructured data
- Facilitates multi-channel consistency
- Facilitates essaging and notification
- Automated tuning: pervasive content can be tuned based on personalization
- Location, browser, etc.
- Integration to other systems

4. KEY FEATURES OF WEB PORTALS

- Security
- Access different data
- Transactions

- Search
- Publish Content
- Personal Content

5. WHAT A WEB PORTAL IS NOT?

- It is not just a Website (which is usually characterized by static information)
- It is not just a personalized intranet
- It is not just a personalized extranet
- It is not just a personalized front end for business applications
- It is not just groupware
- It is not just a personalized knowledge management solution
- It is not just a sophisticated search engine

Instead, a portal is nothing less than just one personalizable, browser-based user interface to all the components mentioned above.

6. MAJOR FUNCTIONS OF WEB PORTALS

According to the analyst and consulting company Ovum—as described in their study "Enterprise Portals: New Strategies for Information Deliver", 2000—the ideal portal is based on eight functionality areas:

- Search and navigation
- Information integration (content management)
- Personalization
- Notification (push technology)
- Task management and workflow
- Collaboration and groupware
- Integration of applications and business intelligence
- Infrastructure functionality

Although most of the functionality is not new, what is new is the idea that the business value of the whole is considerably more than the sum of its parts. Thus, a successful portal does not only consist of either a good collaboration support or a good integration of the information sources. Rather it consists of—just like a successful cooking recipe—a well-integrated mixture of the basic portal functionalities. The first three important functions are explained below.

7. SEARCH AND NAVIGATION

This functionality forms the basis for most of the successful public web portals meaning that a successful portal should support its users in an efficient search for contents.

A Web portal should :

- Automatically present its users with the information appropriate to the user's role.
- Suggest additional information to the user, and/or allow the user to voluntarily personalize the information presented by the portal.
- Allow the user to search for information that was not previously known to be relevant to the user's role, but which may be available through the portal.

QUESTIONS

1. What a web portal does?
2. Discuss the key features of web portals.
3. What a web portal is not?
4. Explain in detail some of the major functions of web portals.
5. Differentiate search and navigation.

6

Web Resources in Library Information Science

1. OBJECTIVES

After studying this lesson, you should be able to:

- Understanding the overview of internet technology
- Different types of internet connectivity
- Describe various types of Web resources
- Different types Browsers, search engines
- Identify the different types of Internet Tools

2. INTRODUCTION

In the 20th century, the world has experienced two revolutions viz. the industrial revolution and the information (technology) revolution due to evolutionary changes in the field of Information technology. Tremendous growth and diversification of knowledge have emerged with multidisciplinary subjects. Information has been identified as one of the vital resources needed for the success in almost every major human endeavor. Collection, organisation and dissemination of information system with economy and efficiency depend on the skills and expertise of the librarians. Information is needed in all aspects of society and in all disciplines. Users demand information, i.e. timely, accurate, valuable, up to date and quickly available.

3. INFORMATION SOURCES OVER THE WEB

- Electronic Journals
- Electronic Discussion Lists/Forums
- Usenet News
- Data and Software Archives
- E-mail-based Information Services
- Campus Wide Information Systems
- Library Catalogues—Web OPACs
- Online Databases
- Guides to Information Sources
- Search Engines
- Subject Gateways
- Web Directories
- Online Chatting
- Commercial Advertisings and Customer Service Information
- Organisations' Directories
- Bulletin Board Services
- Full text of documents

4. TYPES OF WEB RESOURCES

1. **Open Web**—Any thing online that can be found **freely** with a Search Engine
2. **Gated Web**—Online Resources accessible by **Subscription,** e.g. OED, CA, LISA, BIOSIS, INSPEC. COMPENDIX, etc.
3. **Invisible Web**—Databases that **are not found** by Search Engines and can only be accessible through a

particular page or front end. E.g. LC's American Web Site http ://memory• loc.org

5. MEANS OF ACCESS TO WEB RESOURCES

1. Through Search Engines
2. Through Web OPACs
3. Through Specified URLs/Web sites

1. Through Search Engines

- Yahoo http://www.yahoo.com
- Altavista http://www.altavista.com
- Lycos http://www.lycos.com
- Google http://www.google.com
- Excite hltp://www.excite.com
- Hotbot http://www.hotbot.com

6. WEB RESOURCES: VENDOR-WISE

1. IEL Online (http:WleeexpJore.lee.org)

- IEEE/IEE Electronic Library (IEL) provides a single source to almost of the world's current electrical engineering and computer science literature.
- Grants unparalleled access to publications from the Institute of Electrical and Electronics (IEEE) and the Institution of Electrical Engineers (1EE).
- Cover more than 780,000 documents from over 12,000 publications, including, journals, conference proceedings, and IEEE standards.
- Provides access to more than two million full-page PDF images.
- Resources 110 Journals, transactions, magazines, conference proceedings, standards.
- Back-files 1988 onwards.
- Archival Access on DVD at 5% of prevailing subscription rates.

2. Elsevier's Science Direct (http://www.sciencedirect.com)

- **Science Direct** is the web-based interface to the full-text database of Elsevier Science journals
- One of the world's largest providers of scientific, technical and medical literature.
- Offers a rich electronic environment for research journals, bibliographic databases and reference works.
- Offers more than 1500 scientific, technical, medical peer reviewed journals, over 59 million abstracts, over two million full-text scientific journals articles, an expanding suite of bibliographic databases.
- Linking to another one million full-text articles via cross reference to other publisher's platforms.
- Resources 1500 Journals published by Elsevier Science and Academic Press.
- Participants are required to maintain their print Subscription.
- Back-files 1995 onwards.
- Archival Access offered on the cost of preparing set.

3. Springer Verlag's Link (http://link.springe.de)

- Springer Verlag's Link provides Web-based full-text access to the scientific journals published by the Springer Verlag.
- Incorporates full-text of more than 450 journals, several thousand books and other serial publications.
- Offers full-text access to complete collection of their electronic journals (approximately 400) excluding journals in medical science with restrictions in number of downloads limited to maximum of 2,000.
- Well known series of titles like Lecture Notes in Computer Sciences, Physics, Mathematics, etc., in the e-book collection.
- Famous series of e-reference books like Advances in Polymer Science, Landolt-Bornstein Series are available.

- Institutions are required to maintain their print subscription.
- Deletion of subscribed titles not allowed.
- Back-files 1980 onwards.
- Archival Access offered on one time fee of Euro 15,000.

4. ACM Digital Library (http://portal.acm.org/portal.cfm)

- ACM digital library incorporates digital versions of works published by ACM since its inception.
- Nearly half a century of pioneering concepts and fundamental research have been digitized and indexed in a variety of ways in this resource.
- Major components of the resources are an enhanced version of the ACM digital library plus an extended bibliographic database consisting initially of more than a quarter-million citations of crore works in computing.
- Covers works are of all types (journal, proceedings, books, technical reports, theses, among others), and from all the major publishers in the discipline.
- Resources would be accessible through the Web site of ACM digital library.
- Resources 30 full-text Journals, conference proceedings and others.
- No Print-base.
- Web media with CD ROM backup.
- Back-files since inception.
- Archival Access on CD ROM.

5. Ei Compendex plus and INSPEC (http://www.engineeringvillage2.org)

- Ei compendex provides summaries of technical reports, journals articles, and conference papers and proceedings.
- It is the world's only fully interdisciplinary

engineering indexing and abstracting service. It covers over 2,600 international engineering journals, conference proceedings and technical reports.

- Each year, 200,000 new abstracts are added with in the broad applied engineering areas of mechanical, civil, environmental, electrical, structural, process, material science, solid state and super conductivity, bioengineering, energy, chemical, optics, air and water pollution, solid waste management, and road transportation.

6. Knit-Rider Information Services Inc., (DIALOG) http://www.dialog.com

Serving since 1972.

Covers about 400 databases.

One stop service for all the information needs.

Areas covered: Agriculture; Food and Nutrition; Chemistry; Biosciences and Technology; Engineering; Business and Information; Company Information and Financial Data; Computers and Software; Physical Sciences; Energy and Environment; Industry Analysis; Government and Public Affairs; Travel; Medicine, Health Care ad Drug Information; Patents, Trademarks and Copyrights; People, Books and Consumer News; Social Sciences and Humanities.

Products: DIALOG Business Connection (DBC); DAILMAIL; DIALOG Alert; DIAL Order; DIALINDEX; One Search; DIALOG on Disc; DIALOGLink.

7. Silver Platter http://www.silverplater.com

- *Covers about 180 databases.*
- **Areas covered:** Education; Food and Agriculture; Social Sciences; Science and Technology; Health Sciences; Business; Humanities; Environment; Ref. Sources.
- Provides world-wide access to electronic information sources.

8. Proquest Databases (UMI) URL: http://www.umi.com

- 1938—Universal Microfilm International.
- Areas covered: Business; scientific; Technical; humanities; General reference.
- **Products:** Abstract and Index databases; Full Text Databases; Full Image Databases.
- UMI Document Delivery Services: Supply of articles reprints; Supply of reprints of theses

9. ADONIS (Advanced Document Over Network Information Services)

- Covers about 650 journals from 40 publishers.
- Covers Biomedicine, Bioengineering, Biochemistry, Biotechnology.
- Supplies weekly new CDRom to the subscribers of this service, which covers all articles in the fields covered.

10. EEVL—Edinburgh Engineering Virtual Library

- EEVL provides a central access point to networked engineering information for the UK higher education and research community.
- It is a free service, created and run by a team of information specialists from Heriot-Watt University, with input from many other UK universities.
- EEVL covers a Catalogue of selected engineering resources, targeted engineering search engines.

11. The CORE Project

- Chemical Online Retrieval Experiment [CORE] at Cornell University Mannis library.
- Started by American Chemical Society with OCLC.
- Provide access via electronically to all the journals of ACS.

12. IEEE/IEE Electronic Library

- Joint venture by Institute of Electrical and Electronics Engineers (USA) and Institute of Electrical Engineers (UK).
- Covers records from INSPEC database.
- Covers IEEE/IEE Journals, Conference Proceedings standards etc.
- Adds 25,000 (approx.) records per year.
- **Fields covered:** Electrical Engineering; Electronics; IT; Cornputer science; applied Physics and related areas.
- Subscribers will get monthly updates.

13. American Chemical Society

- First professional association to bring electronic form of its 28 periodicals in full text over Bibliographical Retrieval Service (BRS) in 1983.
- By 1993, there were 6998 online ND cd Rom databases

14. Institute of Scientific Information (ISI)

http://www.isinetcom is the site for the Institute for Scientific Information, Philadelphia that has fully integrated e-information solutions. Following details can be obtained while accessing this site:

About ISI
Company Information
Journal Lists
News
ISI Staff Articles
Search
Employment
Training and Support
ISI Links, etc.

ISI Chemistry is a web-based source of information on

new synthetic methods and novel organic compounds. ISI Chemistry delivers the same content publishing in Index Chemistry (IC) and Current Chemical Reactions (CCR) in an easy to read format with advanced searching capabilities.

CCR contains approximately 6,24,000 reactions abstracted from journal articles since 1985 onwards. CCR is updated by 3,000 reactions each month. IC contains approximately 1.4 million compounds abstracted from journal articles from 1996 onwards. 3,500 compounds update it each week.

15. J-Gate http://www.informindia.co.in

- India's first global e-journal portal.
- J-Gate offers around 3 million articles since 2001
- No. of Journals covered is about 10,000
- No. of articles indexed is about 28 lakhs
- No. of articles added each week is about 20,000
- No. of free full text access journals covered is about 1,600
- No. of free full text articles indexed and linked is about 4 lakhs
- No. of articles with author e-mail address is about 9 lakhs

7. WEB RESOURCES : SUBJECT-WISE

1. Engineering Sciences

In the **field** of **Engineering Sciences** the following URLs can be accessed for web-based resources:

www.library.ucsb.edu/subj/enqineer.html. By this web site databases like Compendex Plus, Computer Article Database, Current Contents, IN SPEC, Magazine and Journal Articles, etc. are accessibile. Also accessibility to Newsgroups, Organisations are possible..

http://bubl.ac.ukllink/enqineerinqlinks.html. By this one can access the BUBL link with other accessibility like Edinburg Engineering Virtual Library, and the Databases on Engineering of different disciplines.

http://www2.widener.edul W0Ifqram-M...ary/subject guides/enqineerinq.htm_where one can get the selected resources for Engineering Research which is more useful for doing research activity.

In the field of **Chemical Sciences** the following URLs can be accessed for web based resources:

http://www.cas.orq/This web site is from Chemical Abstracts Service provider. CAS is the producer of the world's largest and most comprehensive databases of chemical information. This covers Chemical Abstracts and Registry. CAS also produces databases of chemical reactions, commercially available chemicals, listed regulated chemicals and compounds claimed in patents. http://pubs.acs.orq/_This site is from the American Chemical Society (ACS) who is the largest producer of Chemical information in the world. One can see the 3 Jist of journals published by the ACS and can search them. Some are freely available with contents.

2. Medical Sciences

In the field of **Medical** Sciences the following URLs can be accessed for web-based resources:

http://www.nih.qov/This site is from the U.S. Department of Health and Human Services. One can get information about publications, fact sheets, clinical trials, grants and funding opportunities, sciertrific resources, etc. by accessing this site.

http://www.nlm.nih.gov This site is from the U.S. National Library of Medicine, wherein one can get information related to MEDL1NE, accessing could download MEDLINEplus, Library Services like catalog, databases, publications, etc. and other information.

http://www.ncbi.nlm.nih.gov/This site is from the National Centre for Biotechnology Information. It acts as a national resource for molecular biology information. Creates databases, conducts research in computational technology, develops software,etc. it related areas.

http://www.healthseek.com/This site is popular for healthcare community and used by hundreds of care giving professionals, medical patients, consumers and ordinary people. Many other web sites can also reached thru[1] this site, as it has linkages to them.

http://avurvedaindia.orq/This is launched recently by the Capital-based NGO Ashtvaidyam Ayurveda Foundation in New Delhi, which explains the fundamental of Ayurveda to the layman in plain and simple language. It is to spread the knowledge of our ancient sciences among the masses.

3. Mathematical Sciences

In the field of **Mathematical Sciences** the following URL can be accessed for web-based resources: .

http://www.emis.de/This is a-site for accessing the European Mathematical Information Service offered by European Mathematical Society. One can access the European countries as well as other countries.

http://www.emis.de/journals This is a site for Mathematicians, wherein they get the list of journals in Mathematics. They will be able to see the contents pages of e-journals among them.

4. Social Sciences

In the field of **Social Sciences** the following URLs can be accessed for web-based resources:

http://www.ssm.com/This is a site for Social Science Research Network, devoted to the worldwide dissemination of social science research and is composed of a number of specialized research networks in each of the social sciences.

QUESTIONS

1. Discuss on the Information Sources over the Web.
2. Specify the types of Web Resources.
3. Write about the Means to access to Web Resources.
4. List out some Web Resources.

PART III

Browsers and Search Engines

Types of Browsers and their Description

1. OBJECTIVES

- Understanding the concept of web browsers
- Different functions of web browsers
- Describe various types of Web resources
- Different types of Browsers, search engines
- Identify the different types of Internet Tools

2. BROWSERS—INTRODUCTORY CONCEPT

Web browser, also called a "browser", to access content published on a web server. Web browsers are software programs that allow accessing the graphical portion of the Internet. Browsers allow the users to access various web sites and view the web pages. They provide the option of entering the URL of the site to be visited. Browser software can be divided into the following two categories:

- Text-based browsers—Lynx

- GUI-based browsers—NCSA Mosaic, Netscape Navigator, Internet Explore, etc.

A browser is an application program that provides a way to look at and interact with all the information on the World Wide Web. The word "browser" seems to have originated prior to the Web as a generic term for user interfaces that let you browse (navigate through and read) text files online. By the time the first Web browser with a graphical user interface was generally available (Mosaic, in 1993), the term seemed to apply to Web content, too. Technically, a Web browser is a client program that uses the Hypertext Transfer Protocol (HTTP) to make requests of Web servers throughout the Internet on behalf of the browser user.

3. FUNCTIONS OF BROWSERS

While some browsers also support e-mail (indirectly through e-mail Web sites) and the File Transfer Protocol (FTP), a Web browser is not required for those Internet protocols and more specialized client programs are more popular.

Short for *Web browser*, a software application used to locate and display Web pages. The two most popular browsers are Netscape Navigator and Microsoft Internet Explorer. Both of these are *graphical browsers*, which means that they can display graphics as well as text. In addition, most modern browsers can present multimedia information, including sound and video, though they require plug-ins for some formats.

4. TYPES OF BROWSERS

A commercial version of the original browser, Mosaic, is in use. Many of the user interface features in Mosaic, however, went into the first widely-used browser, Netscape Navigator. Microsoft followed with its Microsoft Internet Explorer. Today, these two browsers are the only two browsers that the vast majority of Internet users are aware of. Although the online services, such as America Online, originally had their own browsers, virtually all now offer the Netscape or Microsoft browser. Lynx is a text-only browser for UNIX shell and VMS users. Another recently offered and well-regarded browser is Opera.

1. Netscape

Netscape, now part of America Online (AOL), is one of the two most popular Web browsers. Currently, almost all Internet users use either Microsoft's Internet Explorer (MSIE) browser or Netscape, and many users use both. Although Netscape was initially the predominant product in terms of usability and number of users, Microsoft's browser is generally considered superior by many users (although many other users see them as roughly equivalent) and has taken a significant lead in usage.

Netscape's browser, called "Navigator," was developed in 1995 by a team led by Marc Andreessen, who created Mosaic, the first Web browser that had a graphical user interface, at the University of Illinois' National Center for Supercomputing Applications (NCSA) in 1993.

The latest version of the Netscape browser can be downloaded from Netscape's Web site at no charge. CD-ROM versions can also be purchased in computer stores and are sometimes distributed freely as promotions.

AOL envisions the Netscape Web site, now transformed into a leading Web portal, as a leading source of revenue through advertising and e-commerce.

2. Mosaic

Mosaic was the first widely-distributed graphical browser or viewer for the World Wide Web. It is usually considered to have been the software that introduced the World Wide Web (and the Internet) to a wide general audience. Once Mosaic was available, the Web virtually exploded in number of users and content sites. (Of course, the software depended on the recent invention of the Hypertext Transfer Protocol by Tim Berners-Lee.)

Mosaic arrived in 1993. Marc Andreessen, then in his early 20s, is credited with inventing or leading the development of Mosaic. He developed it at the National Center for Supercomputing Applications (NCSA) at the

University of Illinois in Urbana, Illinois. Andreessen and others went on to become part of Netscape Communications, originally called Mosaic Communications, that developed one of today's most popular browsers, Netscape (its full name is Netscape Navigator). The original Mosaic, now in a later version, has since been licensed for commercial use and is provided to users by several Internet access providers.

3. Netscape Communicator

Officially called *Netscape Communications Corporation,* Netscape was founded by James H. Clark and Marc Andreessen in 1994 and was acquired by AOL in 1999. It revolutionized the computer software market by giving away for free its popular Navigator Web browser until it had acquired an overwhelming market share for this category of software. This strategy is now used by many other software companies, including Microsoft, which also distributes its Web browser, *Internet Explorer,* for free. The term *Netscape* is often used as the name of the company's browser, not the company itself.

4. Internet Explorer 6

Internet Explorer 6 is a set of core technologies in Microsoft Windows XP Home Edition and Windows XP Professional operating systems that provides enhanced privacy features and a flexible and reliable browsing experience for users s of Windows XP, Windows Millennium Edition (Windows Me), Windows 2000. Windows 98, and Windows NT® 4.0 with Service Pack 6a or later. Whether you are a home user browsing content or getting e-mail on the Web, an IT administrator deploying and maintaining a rich set of Windows Internet technologies, or a Web developer creating Web content, Internet Explorer 6 gives you the freedom to experience the best of the Internet.

This overview describes some of the major features and technologies of Internet Explorer, provides information on how to get the latest version, and offers links to more information so you can start getting more from the Web the way you want.

1. *Features and Technologies of IE 6*

Internet Explorer 6 includes many new and enhanced features that can simplify the daily tasks that you perform, while helping you to maintain the privacy of your personal information on the Web. Here is a quick look at some of the major features of Internet Explorer 6 that help to provide a flexible and reliable browsing experience on the Web.

Flexibility

With new, innovative browser capabilities and teatures such as **Auto Image Resizing, Image Toolbar, Media Bar,** and **Print Preview,** it's easy to manage, save, and print your pictures and other media from Web pages. Features such as **Favorites, Auto Complete, History,** and the **Search Companion** help you quickly find what you need online. And the **customizable browsing layout** makes it easy to change your layout so you can experience the Web the way you want.

Web Privacy

internet Explorer 6 helps you manage your security and privacy preferences while on the Internet with tools that help you safeguard your family's browsing experience. **Manage cookies** to help control the personal information that Web sites collect about you, set different levels of security for different sites on the Web with **Security Zones,** and use **Content Advisor** to help block access to objectionable content. These tools support the Platform for Privacy Preferences (P3P), a technology under development by the World Wide Web Consortium (W3C).

Reliability

Internet Explorer 6 helps deliver a more stable and more reliable web browsing experience. New **fault collection services** help to identify potential problems that need to be fixed in future updates to Windows Internet technologies. Learn more about these and other Internet Explorer features—including the features that help developers build rich.

5. Opera Browser

The Opera browser started out in 1994 as a research

project in Norway's telecom company, Telenor. Independent development was continued by Opera Software ASA in 1995. The firstVpublic release of the Opera Browser was version 2.12 although earlier demo versions have been found and screenshots of the 1.0 version are available on the web.

Opera's co-founder Jon von Tetzchner made the first public announcement of Opera on Usenet on July 14th 1996. He used the following introduction, which after many years of development still capture the core qualities of Opera

Series 1

Though not publicly released there are screenshots of the then-called MultiTorg Opera. It's fun to recognise the features that are still present in Opera's current form. In weblogs across the web evidence of a Multitorg Opera 1.0b4 can be found.

Series 2

The first public versions of Opera was the 2-series. They are of course extremely outdated but test-driving them you can witness the birth of the legend that is called Opera. The oldest version found is a Norwegian demo version of Opera 2.0 which was included with a PC Magazine. It will only load local pages but you can already see a lot of key features that have made Opera famous!

Series 3

The Opera 3 series saw Opera evolve from a geek's tool to a powerful browsing machine with a climax in features, stability and speed with version 3.62. This version is often taken as a standard to which future version of Opera are compared. It was far ahead of its time in CSS support and this browser can still view the web in a surprisingly good way, considering its respectable age.

Series 4

Opera 4 was long-awaited the first browser based on a new cross-platform core which facilitated the release of Opera for different Operating Systems and thus speeding up Project Magic. The core supported more standards such as CSS1. CSS2, HTML4, XML and WML and a new integrated e-mail client was included. The 04 browser was meant as the leap towards the larger public. Unfortunately the earlier versions were very unstable and buggy and didn't do Opera's reputation much good, though the later maintenance release 4.02 was very usable.

Series 5: "The fastest browser on earth"

The 5 series really made the jump to the large public due to the new ad-sponsored version instead of the 30-day trial period. Furthermore Opera 5 was stable and during following releases it gained new features such as the integrated Instant Messaging, the fantastic mouse-gestures, hotlist panels and the integrated search. The 5 series ended with the 5.12 release which is still used by many today.

Series 6: "Simply the best Internet Experience"

The Opera 6 series introduced the long-awaited Unicode support. Also a new SDI/MDI interface was introduced, facilitating the transition from the SDI-browsers to Opera's unfulpraised MDI-interface. During the later bugfix releases the kioskmode was enhanced, the integrated searches became editable and a lot of printing problems were solved. The 6 series has become stable and feature rich and now really has become a serious competitor to NN and Internet Explorer.

Series 7: "Hey Presto!"

Opera 7 has been released in early 2003. It features a brand new rendering engine under the name Presto, which has enhanced and expanded its support for standards and now includes W3C DOM and the Small Screen Rendering technique for handheld devices. The entire interface was redone, making use of a custom cross-platform skinning system which significantly reduced resource usage, and the entire UI is now configurable: keyboard shortcuts, mouse gestures, menus and toolbars! With the new combined SDI/MDI interface the user has even more power at his command and new innovative features such a FastForward, Notes and Slideshow make the user experience even more enjoyable. Opera 7 is definitely the best browser available today!

An especially noteworthy change in Opera 7 is the new mail and news client, called M2. This e-mail client is based on a powerful filtering system and offers revolutionizing mail organizing abilities, which will change the way you handle your e-mail.

QUESTIONS

1. Write the concept of web browsers.
2. What are the functions of web browsers?
3. Describe various types of Web browsers.
4. Different types of Browsers, search engines.
5. Explain any two web browsers.

Types of Search Engines

1. OBJECTIVES

- To present an overview of the concept of Search Engines
- To highlight the features of different search engines
- To offer tips for the effective searching the various search engines
- Different types of search engines

2. INTRODUCTION

As more and more websites maintain their information in databases and support queries on these databases via some queryable objects embedded in web page, it is becoming necessary for the new generation library systems to introduce new ways to capture such web information generated from databases. Many browse the net for some specific information and log out after a couple of hours with information on everything expect what they needed pin-pointedly. Finding the precise information is perhaps even more difficult than finding the proverbial needle in a haystack, if one doesn't know how to. What strikes one clearly is the absence of a central directory on the net that can locate the entire web at any given time. In spite of the various search engines, locating the exact information is often a hit or a miss proposition. This is because various search engines in the web are programmed to seek out new and updated information at periodic time slots. The easiest way to find anything on the Internet is to use a search engine because these index the plethora of documents on the WWW. Many search engine companies also allow webmasters to submit their homepage for cataloguing by that search engine. This allows the search engine to list the web page. A search engine continuously sends out the so-called spiders, which start on a homepage of a server and pursue all links stepwise. Word indices are created from individual pages and the database is updated.

3. WHAT IS SEARCH ENGINES?

Search engines searches the web. Allows users to enter search terms—keywords/phrases—that are run against a database containing information on the web pages collected automatically by programs called spiders. Retrieves information/web pages from its database that match the search terms entered by searcher. They run from special sites on the web and are designed to help people find information stored on other sites. They differ in their search speed, the design of the search interface, the way in which they display the search results, the amount of help available and so on. They are known by names 'Internet Search Engines' or 'Web Search Engines'.

Search engines have 3 parts.

- Spider/crawler
- Index
- Software/Interface

Although search engines differ in working, the common basic three tasks are: > The search the Internet or select parts of Internet, based on a set of criteria.

- The keep an index of words/phrases they find, with specific information such as where they found them, how many times they found them etc.
- They allow users to search for words/phrases or combination of words/phrases found in that index.
- They are most fascinating information retrieval tools.

4. TYPES OF SEARCH ENGINES

Search engines can be classified as follows:

- Free text search engines—eg. Alta Vista, Lycos, etc.
- Index—or directory-based search engines—eg. Yahoo
- Multi—or meta-search engines—eg. Scurch.com, Vivisimo.com
- Natural language search engines—eg. Aj.com, ask.co.uk
- Resource—or site specific search engines

These search engines can also be classified as follows:

- Major search engines—Google, Yahoo
- News search engines—Newslndex, InfoGrid
- Specialty search engines—Ask Jeeves, Web Help
- Kids search engines—AOL Kids only, KidsClick, Yahooligans
- Metacrawlers—Dogpile, Metacrawler, Cnet Search
- Multimedia search engines—MP3.com, Audiogalaxy
- Regional search engine—Mosaique, Indiainfo.com, Japanese search engines
- Search utilities—Copernic, InfoSeek Express, Lexibot.

5. MAJOR SEARCH ENGINES AND THEIR FEATURES

AltaVista—www.altavista. com

- Word phrase and natural language search facilities.
- Simple and advanced search
- Special search for image, audio-video records.
- Browsing—A no. of categories available.

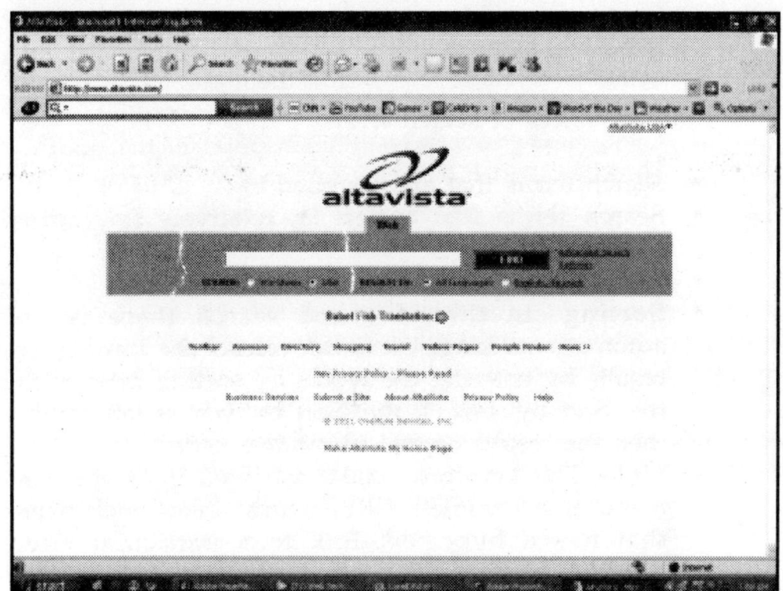

- Supports multilingual search.
- Boolean search using AND, OR, NOT.
- +, – used to indicate that the following search must or must not appear.
- ( ) for nested Boolean search.
- **Proximity search**—NEAR find documents containing both specified words and phrases within 10 words of each other.
- **Truncation—x** is used as a truncation operator that stands for 0-5 characters and can be used only after 3 characters.
- **Phrase search**—A phrase is to be entered within double quotes.
- **Meta-tag search**—Possible on anchor; applet; domain; host; image; like; link; text; title and URL.
- Searches can be limited by language and date.
- **Translate**—Automatic translation of web pages from selected language is available.
- **Family filter**—Can be turned on/off to allow/avoid retrieval of unwanted materials.

- **Ranking**—Result pages are considered more relevant if they have:

More instances of search terms:

- Search terms that are preceded b+;
- Search terms that appear in relatively few other pages.
- Search terms that are closer/together in text.
- **Sorting**—In the advanced search there is no automatic ranking. Users can control the ranking of results by entering the words by sorting them with the 'Sort by' box. If the 'Sort by' box is left blank, then the results appear in random order.
- **Link**—The keyword 'Link:' followed by a domain name or a complete URL, returns every web page that has a hypertext link to a particular site, directory or page.
- Created by Digital Equipment Corporation.
- Provides access to the largest web index by tapping into over 30 million ages, 4 million articles, etc.
- Accessible through any standard web browser.

The screen output of the search engine (www.altavista.com) is shown below:

Excite—www.excite.com

- Words, phrases and natural language queries.
- Special and advanced search options.
- A no. of categories available for browsing.
- Supports multilingual search. Users can search a specific language.
- **Boolean search**—AND, OR, and NOT; + and – signs are used to indicate that the search term following must or must not appear. Parenthesis can be used for Nested Boolean Search.
- **Phrase search**—A phrase is to be entered within double quotes.

- Searches can be limited by language, domain and country.
- Ranking is based on the content of the web pages; their Meta tags; referring anchor text and link popularity.
- If the 'View by URL' option is chosen, then the output will compress to display web site titles and relevant documents contained within the sites.
- The 'Show summaries' option displays the site search results.

The Screen Output of the Search Engine (www.excite.com)

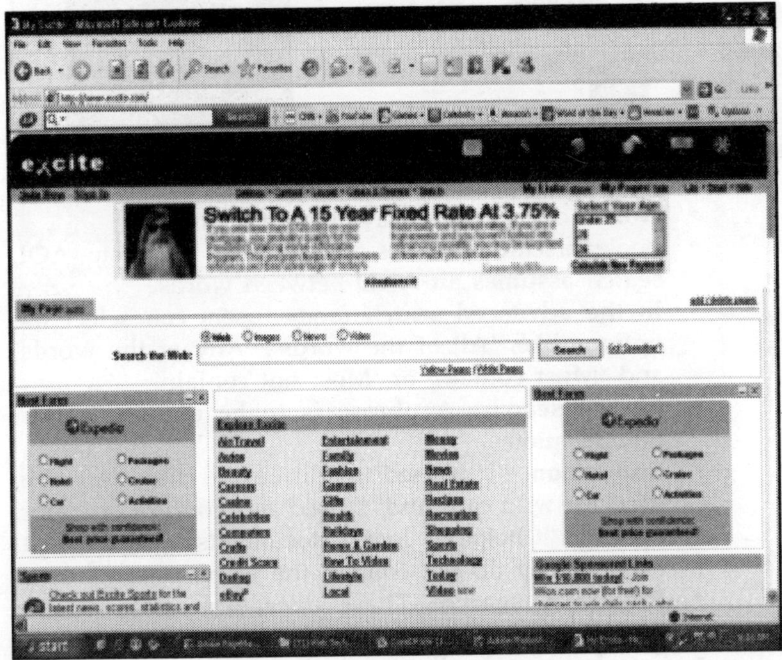

AOL-www.aol.com

- Words, phrases and natural language queries.
- Simple and advanced search options. Special search for news, photo and audio search.

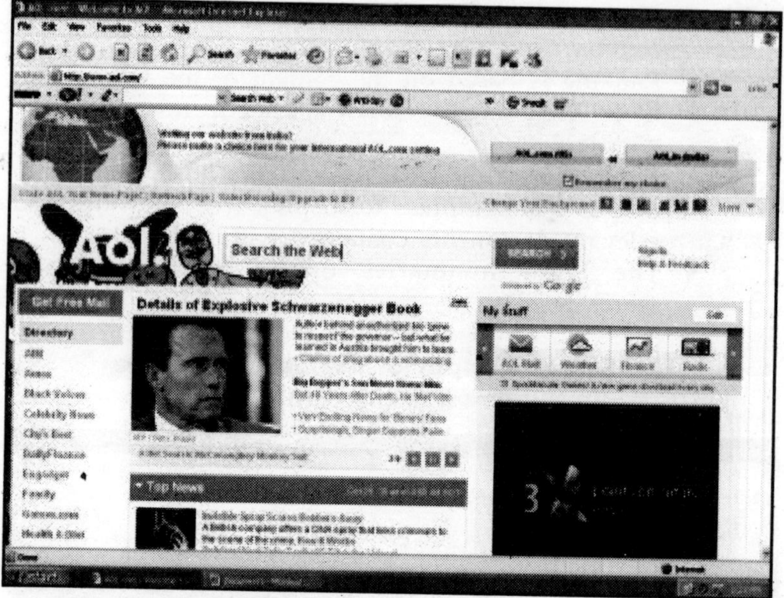

- No. of categories are available for queries.
- Boolean search features are same like AltaVista. AOL search assumes an AND between words.
- In the advanced search mode, users can select the options like, 'All of the words', 'Any of the words' and 'Must contain' or 'Most not contain'.
- **Phrase search**—A phrase is to be entered within double quotes.
- **Truncation**—'?' is used to relpace one character, 'x' is used for wild card and '!' used as a concept operator. For e.g. '!' helps to locate documents on a concept, even if they do not contain the word.
- **Proximity search**—These operators are available namely, ADJ, W/n, and NEAR/m.
- Searches can be limited by language, domain and country.
- H01.COM: Your H,,h Speed Internet Swvke PrOvXiM S«h TopSpeiaU AOL Membe rs, Sign On Access e-nsd, (M, rwsv-i, etc. Introducing AOL* TopSpeed Technology.

Google—www.google.com

- Words and phrases search facilities are available.
- Simple and advanced search options.
- A separate link for Google directory gives access to several browsable categories.
- Supports multilingual search. Users can search in a specific language.
- Boolean search.
- **Phrase search**—A phrase is to be entered within double quotes.
- Searches can be limited by language, link and site.
- **Stopwords**—Searchers can use the '+' sign to include stop words in their search.
- **I'm feeling lucky option**—This option automatically takes the searcher directly to the first web page Google returned for the query.

The Screen Output of the Search Engine (www.google.com)

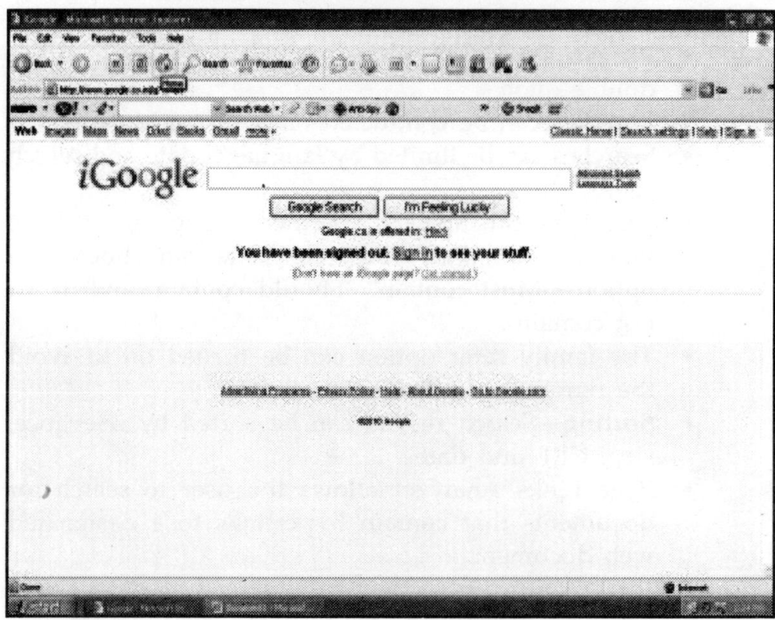

- **Statistics Bar**—This line describes the search and indicates the no. of results returned as well as the amount of time it took to complete the search.
- Ranks pages according to relevance, no. of times sites are visited, etc.
- Google search facilities can easily be added to the user's web browser.
- It makes suggestions for, should spelling mistakes occur.

HotBot—www.hotbot.com

- Quick, advanced, multimedia and director search facilities are available.
- Words and phrase search options available.
- A no. of categories are available for browsing.
- Supports multilingual search. Users can search in a specific language.
- Boolean search.
- **Truncation**—Word stemming option can be activated in the advanced search mode x.
- **Phrase search**—A phrase is to be entered within double quotes.
- Searches can be conducted on a no. of Meta tags.
- Searches can be limited by language, date and search sites.
- Searchers can specify whether a page must have video, audio, PDF files, etc. One can choose the option—'Must contain', 'Should contain' and 'Must not contain'.
- The family filter option can be turned on to avoid the retrieval of offensive materials.
- **Sorting**—Search results can be sorted by relevance, size, URL and date.
- Page Links Analyzer allows the user to search for documents that contain hyperlinks to a designated web document.

Special Commands

- To restrict the search.
- To look for special types of materials on page.
- Restrict a search to the domain selected.

The Screen Output of the Search Engine (www.hotbot.com)

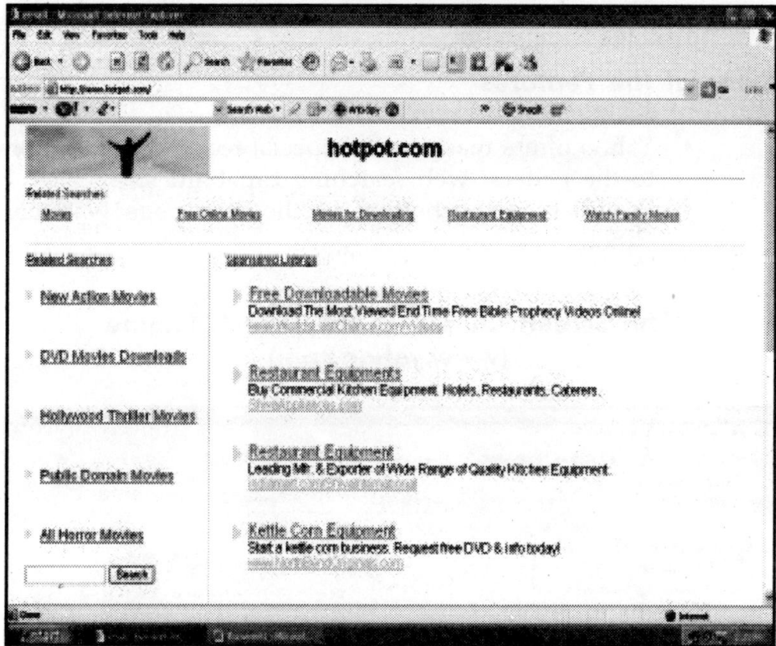

YAHOO www.yahoo.com

Yahoo is one of the most popular hierarchical directories and it is a good starting point. It is well known, well used and well understandable. Yahoo relatively small database each selected by Yahoo staff and assigned a subject classification. Although its slant not scholarly, its selectivity can provide an excellent introduction into topics widely covered on the WWW. It works well when searching is on general information on a subject but may not get when you search for specific subject.

If the search is too specific or esoteric for Yahoo, the search is automatically recycled into Alta Vista's much larger database. One always gets some results either from Yahoo or AltaVista. When a search is automatically submitted to AltaVista, the results from AltaVista are from its simple search. When this happens it is recommended to work/search with AltaVista advanced search.

Yahoo's INDICES are an excellent way to find pages of full links on a topic. Search any term followed by indices and scroll through the results.

Some of the Features

- Yahoo offers many useful special features in addition to the general web searching capabilities.
- Provides at the bottom of the web page National yahoos.

The Screen Output of the Search Engine (www.yahoo.com)

- Provides information for a variety of items such as Libraries, government information, maps, tours which can be searched from the web page itself.
- One can customize a MY YAHOO with the web pages, news and stocks.
- Variety of Searching instructions are provided such as—Phrase searching and Truncation.
- Use of + and—are recommended for the requirements and exclusions.
- Limiting to specific fields in searching.
- Considers case and accent insensitivity.
- Makes possible for sub-searching.

Basically Yahoo is not a search engine, it is a database of links to web and Internet sources organised as a hierarchical subject-oriented guide, commonly known as a catalogue or web directory. It has been divided into 14 broad categories including arts, sciences, business, economy, education, health, reference and government, etc.

Infoseek www.infoseek.com (www.go.com)

Infoseek is one of the best tools for comprehensive searches. It covers about 30 millions sites in full text and searches by keywords. A variety of databases can be searched through Infoseek such as usenet, email addresses, timely news or Web FAQs. It groups web sites into categories.

Important Features

- The search can be narrowed before we use search index by selecting sub-topic.
- The default is Boolean OR but it allows variations of AND, NOT.
- ADJACENT and NEAR.
- Considers capital letter sensitivity.
- Phrase search is possible by enclosing the term in ""quotations".
- The plus sign indicates inclusion of a phrase or word and—minus sign.
- Indicates exclusion.

- Brackets around a word will retrieve words with in 100 words.

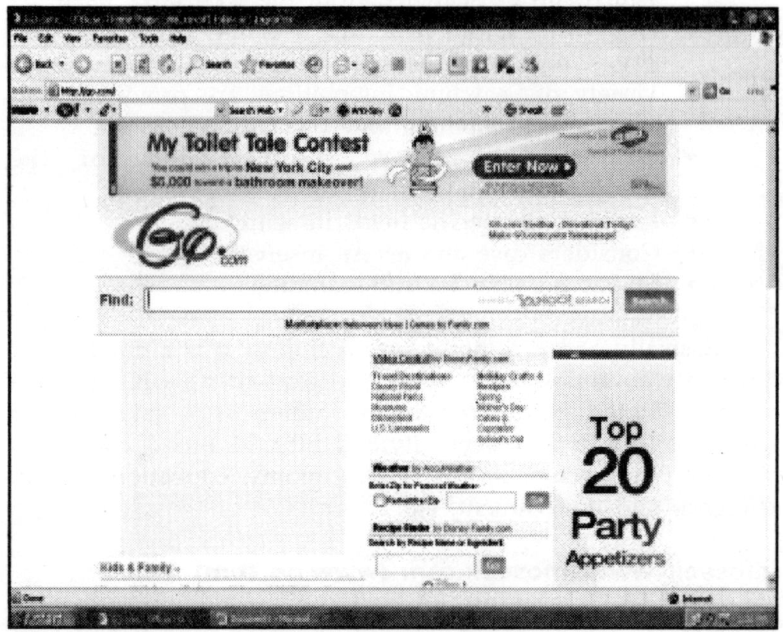

Lycos www.lycos.com

Lycos is one of the first search engines developed for the net. It is a web-indexing robot covering over 55 million URLs of the web. Some of the features are:

- Offers both simple and advanced searches.
- Search by keyword assigns a percentage rating for relevancy of each search term.
- Has the ability to locate GIF, JPEG, and MPEG for pictures and sounds on the Web.
- Has jumped on the channel bandwagon, offering listings grouped by category.
- Offers 18 topical guides accessible from its search from pages.
- It does not permit the use of Boolean operators or nested search logic.

- No mechanism for direct proximity searching using bound phrases or proximity operators.
- Allows uses to govern the closeness among the terms entered
- It is considerably less precise.
- Use of plus (+) sign to include and minus (–) sign to eliminate words is possible.
- Truncation is automatic.

Infoseek boasts ESP or Extra Search Precision, which claims to "intuit" what one. wants in searches of one or two commonly used terms. It searches WebPages, Gopher sites, FTP and Infoseek select sites. It is often praised as the most "precise" of the general web searching tools available.

The Screen Output of the Search Engine (www.lycos.com)

META SEARCH ENGINES

Meta search engines are a combination of a number of search engines and they simultaneously search the multiple search engines. They are also referred to as Parallel search engines, mega search engines or Combined search engines. They do not have their own databases of web pages. They all search most of the popular search engines.

Basic Principles of Meta Search Engines

The Search engines acts depending on certain principles like:

- Accept the user query;
- Convert the query into the correct syntax for every underlying search engine;
- Launch the multiple queries;
- Wait for result;
- Analyze the results, eliminate duplicates, do a ranking;
- Merge the results; and
- Deliver the post-processed result to the users.

Meta search engines do not return all the results retrieved from the individual engines they search. However, the searches they do return are drawn from the top of search engine lists, and therefore tend to be more relevant. Meta search engines are useful in obtaining a quick overview on a subject and/or unique term. Meta search engines are useful in obtaining a quick overview on a subject and/or unique term.

Some of the Meta Search Engines

Dogpile: This engine lives up to its name by virtue of the fact that it searches 25 different Internet search engines such as: AltaVista, Excite, Lycos, InfoSeek, WebCrawler, Thunderstone, Planet Search and Yahoo. For UseNet searching it goes through DejaNews, Reference, AltaVista, and what has become known as the DejaNews old database. It looks for file transfer protocols locales it searches through Filez, and FTP search. And there is a search through the Internet news wire feed, including Yahoo News Headlines, Excite News and InfoSeek Newswires.

SavvySearch: This is one of the oldest of the meta engines; it was founded in mid-1995 as computer science experiment at Colorado State University.

MetaCrawler: Started as a Master's degree project by University of Washington student Erik Selbert 1995, this engine is now operated by the Net company "go2net" which has helped improve an already well-regarded metasearch engine by giving it more infrastructure and tech support.

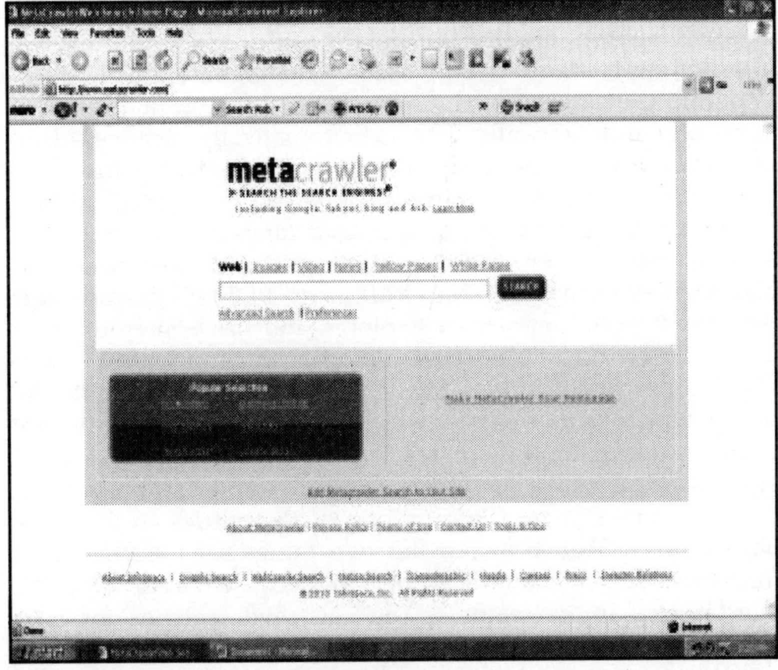

Inference Find http://www.inference.com/ifind/ Active since May of 1995, this is a metasearch engine with the distinction of not listing its findings simply as a lists of hits, but rather it makes "inferences" and arranges findings according to topical subjects.

HuskySearch http://huskysearch.cs.washington.edu As an encore to his development of MetaCrawler, computer science student Erik Selberg, in early 1997 launched this multisearch engine at the University of Washington.

Copernic: Copernic searches the net in an easier, faster and more efficient way than ever. It uses predefined search categories, allowing you to target inquiries to all major Web search engines from various countries, search for relevant text in newsgroups, access popular e-mail directories to find people, compare product prices on auctions sites and search for books, hardware, music, software, and videos in online stores. It provides access to some 80 major information sources. It features a search wizard, the ability to search using a question or keywords, keyword highlighting in results, a detailed search history, automatic software updating via Internet and many useful search management functions. Copernic shows a relevancy score for each result and removes duplicates automatically. It also automatically removes dead links and downloads documents for *off-line browsing* (up to 32 simultaneous transfers). Search results can be viewed off-line, updated and refined using operators (and, or, except, near). Among many other useful features you can save results in various files formats (HTML, XML, text, PDF). Copernic offers integrated tools for Internet Explorer, and has a simple, smart user interface. *Copernic* available on the Weir (www.copernic.com) as a free download and it is similar to such Web pages as Dogpile, which send your search to several engines and gather there results. When the search engines report back, *Copernic* tosses the duplicates and lists the results, ranked by relevance. Click on one of the entries to open the page in your Web browser. But two things set *Copernic* apart from Meta-searches on the Web. First, because it's software, the interface has more features. You can save searches for later use, page through results using a pop-up navigator or e-mail results to a co-worker. It works well with Microsoft and Netscape browsers. Second, the variety of search engines *Copernic* accesses is extensive. The free version combs the Net for e-mail addresses, Usenet messages and Web pages; the Plus version adds more than a dozen topic-specific tools. *Copernic* is also fast on an office network connection; the software gets results in seconds. Even at home on a 28.8k.modem, the results return in about a minute. *Copernic Server* is a powerful Web-based distributed search solution designed for corporate network users. It uses the Copernic.com technology to query hundreds of specialized and multi-language Internet information sources. *Copernic Summarizer,* revolutionary software which is now available to read more in less time by creating concise and accurate summaries. Based on cutting-edge technologies, Copernic Summarizer analyses texts, pinpoints key concepts, and quickly produces summaries composed of the most important sentences.

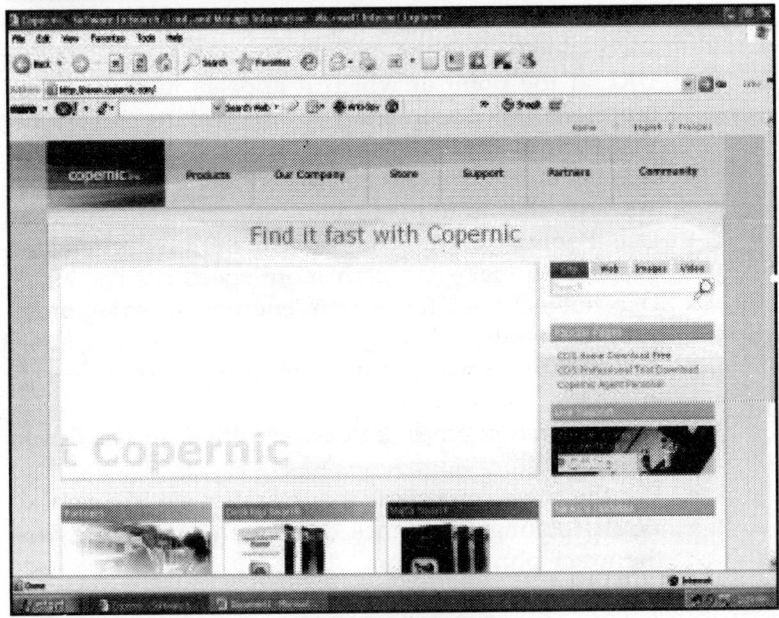

Advantages of Meta Search Engines

The advantages of using Meta Search Engines are :

- Need only access a single web page in order to perform a search.
- Only one interface for searching is to be learned.
- Only one search query is needed to search in many engines.
- More thorough searching across a wider number of search engines.

- We can get an integrated set of results without much duplication.

Tips for Conducting Useful Web Searches

- When you find a useful site, bookmark it.
- Basic knowledge of the way in which URLs are constructed will help you to guess the correct URL for a given web site.
- Often a search will retrieve links to many documents at one site; rather than clicking on each URL in succession to find the desired document, truncate the URL at the point at which it appears most likely to represent the document you are seeking, and type this URL in the location-box of the web browser.
- It is better to do many narrow searches than to make a search that is too broad.
- Use Boolean AND and phrase options whenever possible to make a search more specific.
- Use subject-specific search engines to give more specific results.
- For comprehensive coverage use a Meta search engine.
- Some search engines are case-sensitive, so use lower case letters.
- Put the most important word first in your query.
- While looking for names or something specific, use the exact phrase option.

CONCLUSION

From the above it becomes clear that there are many search engines including Meta search engines that help in exploring the data base in Internet. Search engines are the most fascinating information retrieval tools available free of cost. In order to ensure the timely availability of indigenous and quality data, libraries shall be modified as Digital Libraries and should have Internet Connections.

QUESTIONS

1. What do you mean by Search Engine? Explain the types of Search Engines.
2. State features of YAHOO and AltaVista.
3. Compare the features of Google and Lycos.
4. Briefly describe any four Meta Search Engines.
5. State the tips for the successful surfing of Search Engines.

Search Engines : Function and Evaluation

1. OBJECTIVES

After studying this lesson, you should be able to:

- Present an overview of the concept of Search Engines
- Highlight the features of different search engines
- Offer tips for the effective searching the various search engines
- Different types search engines

2. INTRODUCTION

Today it is estimated that the worldwide, *direct* content availability of more than 150 million documents or pages on more than 650,000 Internet sites. An information server mirroring the entire Internet would require a hard disk capacity on the order of 6 Terabytes (6,000,000,000,000)! Unlike the British Library, the Internet contains material which has not been subjected to any manner of pre-publication review or authentication.

Given the anarchic nature of the Internet, the acquisition, cataloging and authentication of materials is a task which defies description. For example, some 1995 research showed that the average time a page of text remained unchanged was only 75 days with a substantial proportion changing every ten days or less. Despite the abundance of chaff, there are informational kernels of wheat which can be identified and examined by any hearing health professional with Internet access, given the proper tools employed in an optimized manner. These tools are known generically as Internet Search Directories or Catalogs and Search Engines. The Internet references cited in this article serve as categorical examples of search tools rather than a comprehensive listing.

3. SEARCH DIRECTORIES

Internet Search directories differ from Search Engines in that they are **topically arranged,** hierarchical listings of URLs (Uniform Resource Locators) **which have been** subjected to some form of hands-on identification for relevance. **This does not imply** any authentication for accuracy. Entries are acquired by **directory staff using** search engines and by URL submissions. The user selects a general topic and then refines the quest by drilling down until a desired level of specificity is achieved. Often a directory site search engine is available to support open text requests for information from within the directory database.

1. Encyclopedic Search Directories

Encyclopedic directories are eclectic with a wide variety of topics and subtopics. The highest repeat usage rate (79%) among ALL Internet search services belongs to the search directory **YAHOO** <www.yahoo.com> *YAHOO* is allegedly acronymic for "Yet Another Hierarchically Organized Oracle" which has 14 major categories and as many as five or more layers of sub-categories. If you use the on-site search form for a specific query, *YAHOO* will first scour its own site for cached references and then give you the option to expand the inquiry using the *AltaVista* (cited below) search engine with a custom facade. Depth and breadth of categorical information on *YAHOO* is generally rated as superior to other search directories. It contains more than 725,000 cataloged sites.

Less comprehensive but still serviceable search directories include **Magellan** <www.mckinley.com> which reviews and rates sites. **A2Z** <www.a2z.lycos.com> is constructed using the *Lycos* search engine spider to seek out the most frequently linked-to sites **on** the 'Net. **Point.Com's Best of the Web** <http://point.lycos.com/categories/> presents a searchable database of the top 5% of annotated websites editorially reviewed, annotated, rated on content, design and overall.

While these directories also have search engine capabilities, the results are often inadequate. For example, a *Magellan* search of the words: *video otoscopy* allegedly produced 55,834 results. Unfortunately, the primary reference **Audiology Forum: Video Otoscopy** <www.li.net/-sullivan/ears.htm> did not appear in the first 100 listings, the highest relevance among which was rated at only 53%. The seventh ranked relevant listing was entitled *"Live nude girls for video conferencing and teleconferencing"*/A search of *"video otoscopy"* (quotation marks concatenating the two-word phrase) produced only 10 references of which the primary site was ranked seventh with a relevance-to-search rating of 47%.

2. Specialized Search Directories

Specialized directories are limited in scope and focus to selected topics, media or database. For example, one of the most comprehensive directory resources for medical and hearing health professionals is **MedMark** <www.medmark.org>. Thirty-two medical specialty areas are listed as well as links to 24 other related medical directory resources. Selecting **"Otorhinolarvngology** <www.medmark.org/orl/> unveils 14 subcategories with hundreds of listings. Headings include Associations/Societies, Centers/Institutes/Labs, Departments/Divisions, Education/Training, for Consumers, General. Guides/Guidelines, Hospitals/Clinics, Images/Atlases, Information Sources, Journals/News/Publications, Lists of Resources, Other Organizations and Programs/Projects. **Health A to Z** <www.healthatoz.com> is a comprehensive consumer-oriented directory of rated sites in the area of health and medicine.

Specific to hearing health professions, the mo.< comprehensive topical directory is maintained by Internet pioneer Judy Kister at Mankato State University, MN. Initiated in 1994, **'Net Connecti > for Communication Disorders and Sciences** <wu[f]w.mankato.msus.edu/dept/comdis/kuster2/welcome.html> has become an Internet benchmark for thoroughness and dedication in taxonomizing Internet references to communication disorders. It is exceptional in the areas of hearing and deafness.

4. SEARCH ENGINES

Search engines differ from directories in that they use mechanisms called "spiders" or "robots" to continuously scour the Internet for textual content with varying degrees of thoroughness. Some **will** access only page titles, some will locate keywords, others will catalog the entire website textual contents. One enters a keyword or words into the engine's search box. The engine then retrieves any and all references to those morphemic identifiers found in its cache and then lists the corresponding URLs. Search results may be displayed by degree of coincidence with the search criteria or relevance. Some sites provide relevancy ratings. Some provide a miniscule text sample from each site. Others provide summaries if available from the selected site.

In informational searches, often one encounters an embarrassment of riches 'combined with a largesse of fool's gold! xMajor search engine sites are now devoting significant developmental energies to strategies for locating and sampling items of relevance and demand rather than cataloging the universe of content. Consequently, arguments can be made both for and against sampling the same query on different major search engines. **Boolean Operators** (Appendix) can be used to hone the search.

1. Open Set Search Engines

In terms of sheer size and power, **AltaVista** <www.altavista.digital.com>, **HotBot**<www.hotbot.com> and

Excite<www.excite.com> can be considered *large* search engines, cataloging 55-110 MILLION pages and "crawling" 3-10 million pages per day. *Medium* search sites, listing between 30 and 50 million entries, include Lycos<www.lycos.com>, **InfoSeek** <www.infoseek.com> and a relatively new engine **Northern Light** www.northemlight.com>.

WebCrawler<www.webcrawler.com> with 2 million entries is considered a *small search engine.* Among the seven, only two *(AltaVista* and *Northern Light)* do NOT 'present some semblance of a subject directory. In reality, the formerly exclusive functions of search engines and search directories appear to be converging over time.

2. Meta-Search Engines

"Simultaneous multiple engine searches" describes the function of META-search engines. The same query is submitted concurrently to a number of search engines. Unfortunately, this typically results in a large amount of duplicate hits denying the user access to advanced query and search-refining features offered by individual engines. Established sites in this category are **MetaCrawler** <www.metacrawler.com> which simultaneously feeds inquiries to *AltaVista, Excite, Lycos, WebCrawler* and *YAHOO* and SavvySearch <www.savvy.cs.colostate.edu:2000/> which accesses nineteen search resources in twenty-four languages.

META-Searches produce a large amount of data which, unless saved as a file, is difficult to cross correlate and update. Programs are now available for the PC □% to perform a META-Search, store, update and display the results, by rank, date or other variable for off-line viewing. A convenient, freeware program for this application is **Copernic 98** <www.copernic.com> sending concurrent requests to 33 leading search engines and directories.

3. Limited Set Search Engines

In this category, search engines are limited in scope to a specific Internet protocol, medium, topic, database, single site or single PC.

4. Internet Protocol-Specific

Search mechanisms described thus far retrieve material via HyperText Transfer Protocol ***(HTTP)***. Other Internet protocols include Network News Transfer Protocol *(NNTP)*; i.e. newsgroup/Usenet postings; and File Transfer Protocol **(FTP)** for accessing downloadable files and programs.

A notable search engine of newsgroup or Usenet postings is DejaNews <www.dejanews.com> indexes more than 50,000 news/discussion groups and archives postings over more than 2.5 years. *AltaVista* and *InfoSeek* both provide NNTP/usenet search options.

A user-friendly search mechanism for file transfer protocol (FTP) downloads is **Jumbo** <www.jumbo.com> with 250,000 downloadable shareware and freeware programs classified in twelve categories.

5. Medium-Specific

This Service has been Discontinued News Works <www.newsworks.com> allows a topical search of 140 newspapers. **MedLine** <www.ncbi.nlm.nih.gov/PubMed> provides search access to references and abstracts of more than 9 million journal citations. E-mail addresses and telephone listings can be located using **Fourll** <www.fourll.com>.

American Directory Assistance and **American Yellow** Pages <www.lookupusa.com> locate private and business telephone listings. An *American Yellow Pages* search on "audiologist" produced no finding in Garden City, NY. A search on "audiologists" or "aud*" produced my office name, address, telephone number, a zoomable street map (locating me three blocks east of where I actually practice) and a "good" credit rating. White page listed telephone numbers can be located via *American Directory Assistance.*

6. Database-Specific

Thomas (Jefferson) <http://thomas.loc.gov> Provides federal legislation information. Complete texts of bills and regulations in both houses of Congress can be searched with current status. Federal regulations through 1973 are indexed and available. The Congressional Record may be accessed as well as Congressional committee information.

A number of states provide similar legislative search capability including **Official California Legislative Information** <www.leginfo.ca.gov> and New **York State Legislature** <http://unix2.nysed.gov/ils/legislature/legis.html>. Large, open set search engines can be used to determine the availability of legislative status information in other states.

While clearly an on-line superstore, **Barnes and** Noble <http://barnesandnoble.com>, provides subject, author and title search capability on millions of titles. An on-site search of "audiology" produced 250 available titles, some at discount. Fewer titles, often at lower prices, were found at Amazon.com <http://amazon.com> and **www.books.com** <www.books.com>. The latter, a fee-for-membership site, provides price comparisons with other on-line bookstores.

7. Site-Specific

Search engines are also applicable to the contextually disparate contents of single websites. Examples of single site search engines can be found at the **American Academy of Audiology** <wwwʳ.audiology.org/search-aaa/> and at the **American Speech-Language Hearing Association** <www.asha.org/search.htm>.

5. HELPFUL TIPS FOR EFFECTIVE SEARCHING

- Use search directories if you want to find information on a general topic. Search engines are best for gathering a universe of information on a highly circumscribed topic.
- Specialized directories with smaller, subject-oriented databases, such as Judy Kusters' website (cited above), tend to produce more valid, up-to-date samples of information.
- Make sure your spelling is correct for search engines. An *AltaVista* search on "cerumin" will produce 12 references, 10 in Spanish or Portuguese and two referring to "cerumin"—as the root for terms such as "ceruminectomy" and "ceruminosis". A search on

"cerumen" produces 770 references. You can monitor on-line search term requests at the *Magellan* **"Search Voyeur"** <voyeur.mckinley.com/cgi-bin/voyeur.cgi>. You will encounter spelling errors within the first two or three minutes.

- Be as specific as possible in your search request. Refining the above *AltaVista* search request to "cerumen management" produced 74 targeted references.
- Use quotation marks for phrases and names. Use capital letters to specify proper names and locations.
- Learn **BOOLEAN OPERATORS** (Appendix), to refine searches as used by the different engines. Consult the engine or directory's HELP resource for details.
- Use multiple browser windows, one for the engine and one to explore sites. In **Netscape Navigator** <www.netscape.com/download/> or **MS Internet Explorer (IE)** <www.microsoft.com/ie/download/>, select "New Window" or "New Browser" from the "file" menu, respectively. *IE version 4.0* presents a "Search" button which places various search engines on the left side of the screen and results on the right. Don't look beyond the first page or two of results. Search again with different keywords. Bookmark sites that look promising. Print out pages on-line for reference or reading when you are not at a computer. Make sure the URL prints on each page for reacquisition. If available as a feature on your search directory or engine, request notification of changes to sites of interest.

6. RECOMMENDED CONTEMPORARY REFERENCES ON SEARCHING THE WORLD WIDE WEB

Internet

Sullivan, D., **Search Engine Watch;** <www.searchenginewatch.com>; 1998.

APPENDIX

BOOLEAN AND OTHER SEARCH OPERATORS

Operator	*Example*	*Application*
And	ear AND infection	Requires bother terms in the document, not necessarily adjacent. Boolean operators must be all in capital letters.
+	+ear + infection	Same as above
"..."	"ear infection"	Requires adjacency of terms in phrase
NOT	+"hearing aid	Will require zinc and "battery" + zinc exclude documents NOT mercury mentioning mercury hearing aid batteries
–	+"hearing aid	Same as above battery"+ zinc – mercury
OR	sensorineural OR "sensory neural"	Acquires documents EITHER or BOTH terms
[no operator]	recruitment "loudness growth"	Same as OR, above
NEAR	Recruitment NEAR	Acquires documents where Compression (in Altavista) one term is within 10 words of the other.
[Nesting]	(analog OR digital) AND Programmable AND "hearing aid"	Without parentheses, the search would be : Analog OR (digital AND Programmable AND "hearing aid"

[Wildcard]	audiolog*	Acquires documents with audiology, audiologist, audiological
[Stopwords]	Portland NEAR "OR" AND Portland NEAR "ME"	Without quotes, engines may ignore OR as a stopword or consider it an operator.
[Case Sensitivity]	AuD OR Au.D.	Forces exact match, ignores auD, AUD, aud, AU.D., etc.

7. CONCLUSION

Searching and retrieving infonnation in the web resources is an art instead of .science. The information thus retrieved by all search engines is not one and the same. Number of hits differs from one search engines to another. Once the searching concept is well understood, the desired information can be retrieved.

QUESTIONS

1. To present an overview of the concept of Search Engines.
2. To highlight the features of different search engines.
3. To offer tips for the effective searching the various search engines.
4. Different types search engines.

PART IV

Web Technology

10

Meta Data

1. OBJECTIVES

- Understanding the concept of meta data
- Define Meta data and Markup
- Differentiate data and meta data
- Describe various types of meta data
- Different types Browsers, search engines
- Describe the Use of meta data
- Identify the important issues of meta data
- Describe the classes of meta data

2. WHAT IS META DATA?

Meta data (meta data, or sometimes metainformation) is "data about data", of any sort in any media. An item of Meta data may describe an individual datum, or content item, or a collection of data including multiple content items.

Meta is a classical Greek preposition (jiet' aXXoov etaipcov) and prefix *(liExafiaoiq)* conveying the following senses in English, depending upon the case of the associated noun: among; along with; with; by means of; in the midst of;

after; behind.[1/1] In epistemology, the word means "about (its own category)": thus Meta data is "data about the data".

Meta data is used to facilitate the understanding, characteristics, and management usage of data. The Meta data required for effective data management varies with the type of data and context of use. In a library, where the data is the content of the titles stocked, Meta data about a title would typically include a description of the content, the author, the publication date and the physical location.

In the context of a camera, where the data is the photographic image, Meta data would typically include the date the photograph was taken and details of the camera settings (lens, focal length, aperture, shutter timing, white balance, etc.). On a digital portable music player, the album names, song titles and album art embedded in the music files are used to generate the artist and song listings, and are considered the meta data.

In the context of an information system, where the data is the content of the computer files, Meta data about an individual data item would typically include the name of the field and its length. Meta data about a collection of data items, a computer file, might typically include the name of the file, the type of file and the name of the data administrator.

1. Examples of Meta Data

Meta data provides context for data.

If we consider a particular place in the real world, this may be described by data, for
example:

1. "E83BJ"
2. "17"
3. "Sunny"

To make sense of and use this data, context is important, and can be provided by meta data. The Meta data for the above three items of data might include:

- 1.1 "Post Code"—This is a brief description (or name) of the data item "E83BJ"

- 1.2 "The unique identifier of a postal district"—This is another description (a definition) of "E83BJ"
- 1.3 "27 June 2006"—This could also help describe "E83BJ", for example by giving the date it was last updated
- 2 "Average temperature in degrees Celsius"—This is a possible description of "17"
- 3 "Yesterday's weather"—This is a description of "sunny"

An item of Meta data is itself data and therefore may have its own meta data. For example, "Post Code" might have the following meta data:

- 1.1.1 "data item name"
- 1.1.2 "5 characters, starting with A-Z"

"27 June 2006" might have the following meta data:

- 1.3.1 "date last changed"
- 1.3.2 "ddMMMyyyy"

The hierarchy of Meta data descriptions can go on forever, but usually context or semantic understanding makes extensively detailed explanations unnecessary.

2. Levels

The role played by any particular datum depends on the context. For example, when considering the geography of London, "E83BJ" would be a datum and "Post Code" would be metadatum. But, when considering the data management of an automated system that manages geographical data, "Post Code" might be a datum and then "data item name" and "5 characters, starting with A-Z" would be meta data. In any particular context, Meta data characterizes the data it describes, not the entity described by that data. So, in relation to "E83BJ", the datum "is in London" is a further description of the place in the real world which has the post code "E83BJ", not of the code itself. Therefore, although it is providing information connected to "E83BJ" (telling us that this is the post code of a place in London), this would not normally be considered meta data, as it is describing "E83BJ" *qua* place in the real world and not *qua* data.

3. Definitions

The term was introduced intuitively, without a formal definition. Because of that, today there are various definitions. The most common one is the literal translation:

- "Data about data are referred to as meta data."^
  Example: "12345" is data, and with no additional context is meaningless. When "12345" is given a meaningful name (meta data) of "ZIP code", one can understand (at least in the United States, and further placing "ZIP code" within the context of a postal address) that "12345" refers to the General Electric plant in Schenectady.
  As for most people the difference between data and information is merely a philosophical one of no relevance in practical use, other definitions are:
- Meta data is information about data.
- Meta data is information about information.
- Meta data contains information about that data or other data.

There are more sophisticated definitions, such as:

- "Meta data is structured, encoded data that describe characteristics of information-bearing entities to aid in the identification, discovery, assessment, and management of the described entities."
- "[Meta data is a set of] optional structured descriptions that are publicly available to explicitly assist in locating objects. "

These are used more rarely because they tend to concentrate on one purpose of Meta data to find "objects", "entities" or "resources" and ignore others, such as using Meta data to optimize compression algorithms, or to perform additional computations using the data.

The Meta data concept has been extended into the world of systems to include any "data about data": the names of tables, columns, programs, and the like. Different views of this "system meta data" are detailed below, but beyond that is the recognition that Meta data can describe all aspects of systems: data, activities, people and organizations involved, locations of data and processes, access methods, limitations, timing and events, as well as motivation and rules.

Fundamentally, then, Meta data is "the data that describe the structure and workings of an organization's use of information, and which describe the systems it uses to manage that information". To do a model of Meta data is to do an "Enterprise model" of the information technology industry itself.

3. META DATA AND MARKUP

In the context of the web and the work of the W3C in providing markup technologies of HTML, XML and SGML the concept of Meta data has specific context that is perhaps clearer than in other information domains. With markup technologies there is meta data, markup and data content. The Meta data describes characteristics about the data, while the markup identifies the specific type of data content and acts as a container for that document instance. This page in Wikipedia is itself an example of such usage, where the textual information is data, how it is packaged, linked, referenced, styled and displayed is markup and aspects and characteristics of that markup are Meta data set globally across Wikipedia.

In the context of markup the Meta data is architected to allow optimization of document instances to contain only a minimum amount of meta data, while the Meta data itself is likely referenced externally such as in a schema definition (XSD) instance. Also it should be noted that markup provides specialised mechanisms that handle referential data, again avoiding confusion over what is Meta data or data, and allowing optimizations. The reference and ID mechanisms in markup allowing reference links between related data items, and links to data items that can then be repeated about a data item, such as an address or product details. These are then all themselves simply more data items and markup instances rather than meta data.

Similarly, there are concepts such as classifications, ontologies and associations for which markup mechanisms are provided. A data item can then be linked to such categories via markup and hence providing a clean delineation between what is meta data, and actual data instances. Therefore the concepts and descriptions in a classification would be meta data, but the actual classification entry for a data item is simply another data instance.

Some examples can illustrate the points here. Items in bold are data content, in italic are meta data, normal text items are all markup.

The two examples show in-line use of Meta data within markup relating to a data instance (XML) compared to simple markup (HTML).

A simple HTML instance example:

<spanstyle="normalText">Example</span> And then a XML instance example with meta data: <PersonMiddle Name *nillable-"true* ">John</PersonMiddleName>

Where the inline assertion that a person's middle name may be an empty data item is Meta data about the data item. Such definitions however are usually not placed inline in XML. Instead these definitions are moved away into the schema definition that contains the Meta data for the entire document instance. This again illustrates another important aspect of Meta data in the context of markup. The Meta data is optimally defined only once for a collection of data instances. Hence repeated items of markup are rarely meta data, but rather more markup data instances themselves.

4. HIERARCHIES OF META DATA

When structured into a hierarchical arrangement, Meta data is more properly called an ontology or schema. Both terms describe "what exists" for some purpose or to enable some action. For instance, the arrangement of subject headings in a library catalog serves not only as a guide to finding books on a particular subject in the stacks, but also as a guide to what subjects "exist" in the library's own ontology and how more specialized topics are related to or derived from the more general subject headings.

Meta data is frequently stored in a central location and used to help organizations standardize their data. This information is typically stored in a Meta data registry.

5. DIFFERENCE BETWEEN DATA AND META DATA

Usually it is not possible to distinguish between (plain) data and Meta data because:

- Something can be data and Meta data at the same time. The headline of an article is both its title (meta data) and part of its text (data).
- Data and Meta data can change their roles. A poem, as such, would be regarded as data, but if there were a song that used it as lyrics, the whole.
- poem could be attached to an audio file of the song as meta data. Thus, the labeling depends on the point of view.

These considerations apply no matter which of the above definitions is considered, except where explicit markup is used to denote what is data and what is meta data.

6. USE OF META DATA

Meta data is used to speed up and enrich searching for resources. In general, search queries using Meta data can save users from performing more complex filter operations manually. It is now common for web browsers (with the notable exception of Mozilla Firefox), P2P applications and media management software to automatically download and locally cache meta data, to improve the speed at which files can be accessed and searched.

Meta data may also be associated to files manually. This is often the case with documents which are scanned into a document storage repository such as FileNet or Documentum. Once the documents have been converted into an electronic format a user brings the image up in a viewer application, manually reads the document and keys values into an online application to be stored in a Meta data repository.

Meta data provide additional information to users of the data it describes. This information may be descriptive ("These pictures were taken by children in the school's third grade class.") or algorithmic ("Checksum^ 39F").

Meta data helps to bridge the semantic gap. By telling a computer how data items are related and how these relations can be evaluated automatically, it becomes possible to process even more complex filter and search operations. For example, if a search engine understands that "Van Gogh" was a "Dutch painter", it can answer a search query on "Dutch painters" with a link to a web page about Vincent Van Gogh, although the exact words "Dutch painters" never occur on that page. This approach, called knowledge representation, is of special interest to the semantic web and artificial intelligence.

Certain Meta data is designed to optimize lossy compression. For example, if a video has Meta data that allows a computer to tell foreground from background, the latter can be compressed more aggressively to achieve a higher compression rate.

Some Meta data is intended to enable variable content presentation. For example, if a picture has Meta data that indicates the most important region—the one where there is a person—an image viewer on a small screen, such as on a mobile phone's, can narrow the picture to that region and thus show the user the most interesting details. A similar kind of Meta data is intended to allow blind people to access diagrams and pictures, by converting them for special output devices or reading their description using text-to-speech software.

Other descriptive Meta data can be used to automate workflows. For example, if a "smart" software tool knows content and structure of data, it can convert it automatically and pass it to another "smart" tool as input. As a result, users save the many copy-and-paste operations required when analyzing data with "dumb" tools.

Meta data is becoming an increasingly important part of electronic discovery. If Application and file system Meta data derived from electronic documents and files can be important evidence. Recent changes to the Federal Rules of Civil Procedure make Meta data routinely discoverable as part of civil litigation. Parties to litigation are required to maintain and produce Meta data as part of discovery, and spoliation of Meta data can lead to sanctions.

Meta data has become important on the World Wide Web because of the need to find useful information from the mass of information available. Manually-created Meta data adds value because it ensures consistency. If a web page about a certain topic contains a word or phrase, then all web pages about that topic should contain that same word or phrase. Meta data also ensures variety, so that if a topic goes by two names each will be used. For example, an article about "sport utility vehicles" would also be tagged "4 wheel drives", "4WDs" and "four wheel drives", as this is how SUVs are known in some countries.

Examples of Meta data for an audio CD include the MusicBrainz project and All Media Guide's Allmusic. Similarly, MP3 files have Meta data tags in a format called ID3.

7. TYPES OF META DATA

Meta Data can be classified

- Content. Meta data can either describe the *resource* itself (for example, name and size of a file) or the *content* of the resource (for example, "This video shows a boy playing football").
- Mutability. With respect to the whole resource, Meta data can be either *immutable* (for example, the "Title" of a video does not change as the video itself is being played) or *mutable* (the "Scene description" does change).
- Logical function. There are three layers of logical function: at the bottom the *subsymbolic* layer that contains the raw data itself, then the *symbolic* layer with Meta data describing the raw data, and on the

top the *logical* layer containing Meta data that allows logical reasoning using the symbolic layer

8. IMPORTANT ISSUES OF META DATA

To successfully develop and use meta data, several important issues should be treated with care:

1. Meta Data Risks

Microsoft Office files include Meta data beyond their printable content, such as the original author's name, the creation date of the document, and the amount of time spent editing it. Unintentional disclosure can be awkward or even, in professional practices requiring confidentiality, raise malpractice concerns. Some of Microsoft Office document's Meta data can be seen by clicking *File* then *Properties* from the program's menu. Other Meta data is not visible except through external analysis of a file, such as is done in forensics. The author of the Microsoft Word-based Melissa computer virus in 1999 was caught due to Word Meta data that uniquely identified the computer used to create the original infected document.

2. Meta Data Lifecycle

Even in the early phases of planning and designing it is necessary to keep track of all Meta data created. It is not economical to start attaching Meta data only after the production process has been completed. For example, if Meta data created by a digital camera at recording time is not stored immediately, it may have to be restored afterwards manually with great effort. Therefore, it is necessary for different groups of resource producers to cooperate using compatible methods and standards.

- Manipulation. Meta data must adapt if the resource it describes changes. It should be merged when two resources are merged. These operations are seldom performed by today's software; for example, image editing programs usually do not keep track of the Exif Meta data created by digital cameras.

- Destruction. It can be useful to keep Meta data even after the resource it describes has been destroyed, for example in change histories within a text document or to archive file deletions due to digital rights management. None of today's Meta data standards consider this phase.

3. Storage of Meta Data

Meta data can be stored either *internally,* in the same file as the data, or *externally,* in a separate file. Meta data that are embedded with content is called *embedded meta data.* A data repository typically stores the Meta data *detached* from the data. Both ways have advantages and disadvantages:

- **Internal storage** allows transferring Meta data together **with** the data it describes; thus, Meta data is always at hand and can be manipulated easily. This method creates high redundancy and does not allow holding Meta data together.
- **External storage** allows bundling meta data, for example in a database, for more efficient searching. There is no redundancy and Meta data can be transferred simultaneously when using streaming. However, as most formats use URIs for that purpose, the method of how the Meta data is linked to its data should be treated with care. What if a resource does not have a URI (resources on a local hard disk or web pages that are created on-the-fly using a content management system)? What if Meta data can only be evaluated if there is a connection to the Web, especially when using RDF? How to realize that a resource is replaced by another with the same name but different content?

  Moreover, there is the question of data format: storing Meta data in a human-readable format such as XML can be useful because users can understand and edit it without specialized tools. On the other hand, these formats are not optimized for storage capacity; it may be useful to store Meta data in a binary, non-human-readable format instead to speed up transfer and save memory.

4. Criticisms on Meta data

Although the majority of computer scientists DEEP""0'7 needed] see Meta data as a chance for better interoperability, some critics argue:

- Meta data is too expensive and time-consuming. The argument is that companies will not produce Meta data without need because it costs extra money, and private users also will not produce complex Meta data because its creation is very time-consuming.
- Meta data is too complicated. Private users will not create Meta data because existing formats, especially MPEG-7, are too complicated. As long as there are no automatic tools for creating meta data, it will not be created.
- Meta data is subjective and depends on context. Most probably, two persons- will attach different Meta data to the same resource due to their different points of view. Moreover, Meta data can be misinterpreted due to its dependency on context. For example, searching for "post-modern art" may miss a certain item because the expression was not in use at the time when **that** work of art was created, or searching for "pictures taken at 1:00" may produce confusing results due to local time differences.
- There is no end to meta data. For example, when annotating a match of soccer with meta data, one can describe all the players and their actions in time and stop there. One can also describe the advertisements in the background and the clothes the players wear. One can also describe each fan on the tribune and the clothes they wear. All of **this** Meta data can be interesting to one party or another—such as the spectators, sponsors or a counter-terrorist unit of the police—and even for a simple resource the amount of possible Meta data can be gigantic.

- Meta data is useless. Many of today's search engines are very efficient at finding text. Other techniques for finding pictures, videos and music (namely query-by-example) will become more and more powerful in the future. Thus, there is no real need for meta data.

The opposers of Meta data sometimes use the term metacrap to refer to the unsolved problems of Meta data in some scenarios. These people are also referred to as "Meta Haters."

9. CLASSES OF META DATA

In general, there are two distinct classes of meta data: structural or control Meta data and guide meta data. Structural Meta data is used to describe the structure of computer systems such as tables, columns and indexes. Guide Meta data is used to help humans find specific items and is usually expressed as a set of keywords in a natural language.

Metatadata can be divided into 3 distinct categories:

- Descriptive
- Administrative
- Structural

1. Relational Database Meta Data

Each relational database system has its own mechanisms for storing meta data. Examples of relational-database Meta data include:

- Tables of all tables in database, their names, sizes and number of rows in each table.
- Tables of columns in each database, what tables they are used in, and the type of data stored in each column.

In database terminology, this set of Meta data is referred to as the catalog. The SQL standard specifies a uniform means to access the catalog, called the INFORMATIONSCHEMA, but not all databases implement it, even if they implement other aspects of the SQL standard. For an example of database-specific Meta data access methods, see Oracle meta data.

2. Data Warehouse Meta Data

Data warehouse Meta data systems are sometimes separated into two sections:

1. **back room** Meta data that are used for Extract, transform, load functions to get OLTP data into a data warehouse, and
2. **front room** Meta data that are used to label screens and create reports Kimball^ lists the following types of Meta data in a data warehouse.

Source system meta data

- source specifications, such as repositories, and source logical schemas,
- source descriptive information, such as ownership descriptions, update frequencies, legal limitations, and access methods, and
- process information, such as job schedules and extraction code.

Data staging meta data

- data acquisition information, such as data transmission scheduling and results, and file usage,
- dimension table management, such as definitions of dimensions, and surrogate key assignments,
- transformation and aggregation, such as data enhancement and mapping, DBMS load scripts, and aggregate definitions, and
- audit, job logs and documentation, such as data lineage records, data transform logs.

DBMS meta data, such as:

- DBMS system table contents
- processing hints

Michael Bracket defines Meta data (what he calls "Data resource data") as "any data about the organization's data resource".^ Adrienne Tannenbaum defines Meta data as "the detailed description of instance data. The format and characteristics of populated instance data: instances and values, dependent on the role of the Meta data recipient".[9] These definitions are characteristic of the "data about data" definition.

3 Business Intelligence Meta Data

Business Intelligence is the process of analyzing large amounts of corporate data, usually stored in large databases such as the Data Warehouse, tracking business performance, detecting patterns and trends, and helping enterprise business users make better decisions. Business Intelligence Meta data describes how data is queried, filtered, analyzed, and displayed in Business Intelligence software tools, such as Reporting tools, OLAP tools, Data Mining tools.

Examples

- **OLAP meta data**: The descriptions and structures of Dimensions, Cubes, Measures (Metrics), Hierarchies, Levels, Drill Paths.
- **Reporting meta data**: The descriptions and structures of Reports, Charts, Queries, DataSets, Filters, Variables, Expressions.
- **Data Mining meta data**: The descriptions and structures of DataSets, Algorithms, Queries.

Business Intelligence Meta data can be used to understand how corporate financial reports reported to Wall Street are calculated, how the revenue, expense and profit are aggregated from individual sales transactions stored in the data warehouse. A good understanding of Business Intelligence Meta data is required to solve complex problems such as compliance with corporate governance standards.

4. General IT Meta Data

In contrast, David Marco, another Meta data theorist,

defines Meta data as "all physical data and knowledge from inside and outside an organization, including % information about the physical data, technical and business processes, rules and constraints of the data, and structures of the data used by a corporation." Others have included web services, systems and interfaces. In fact, the entire Zachman framework.

Notice that such definitions expand meta data's scope considerably, to encompass most or all of the data required by the Management Information Systems capability. In this sense, the concept of Meta data has significant overlaps with the ITIL concept of a Configuration Management Database (CMDB), and also with disciplines such as Enterprise Architecture and IT portfolio management. This broader definition of Meta data has precedent. Third generation corporate repository products (such as those eventually merged into the CA Advantage line) not only store information about data definitions but also about the programs accessing those data structures, and the Job Control Language and batch job infrastructure dependencies as well. These products (some of which are still in production) can provide a very complete picture of a mainframe computing environment, supporting exactly the kinds of impact analysis required for ITIL-based processes such as Incident and Change Management. The ITIL Back Catalogue includes the *Data Management* volume which recognizes the role of these Meta data products on the mainframe, posing the CMDB as the distributed computing equivalent. CMDB vendors however have generally not expanded their scope to include data definitions, and Meta data solutions are also available in the distributed world. Determining the appropriate role and scope for each is thus a challenge for large IT organizations requiring the services of both.

Since Meta data is pervasive, centralized attempts at tracking it need to focus on the most highly leveraged assets. Enterprise Assets may only constitute a small percentage of the entire IT portfolio.

Some practitioners have successfully managed IT Meta data using the Dublin Core metamodel.

5. IT Meta Data Management Products

First generation data dictionary/Meta data repository tools would be those only supporting a specific DBMS, such as IDMS's IDD (integrated data dictionary), the IMS Data Dictionary, and ADABAS's Predict.

Second generation would be ASG's DATAMANAGER product which could support many different file and DBMS types.

Third generation repository products became briefly popular in the early 1990s along with the rise of widespread use of RDBMS engines such as IBM's DB2.

Fourth generation products link the repository **with** more Extract, transform, load tools and can be connected with architectural modeling tools. Examples include

Adaptive Meta data Manager from Adaptive, Rochade from ASGJnfoLibrarian Meta data Integration Framework and Troux Technologies Metis Server product.

6. File System Meta Data

Nearly all file systems keep Meta data about files out-of-band. Some systems keep Meta data in directory entries; others in specialized structure like inodes or even in the name of a file. Meta data can range from simple timestamps, mode bits, and other special-purpose information used by the implementation itself, to icons and free-text comments, to arbitrary attribute-value pairs.

With more complex and open-ended meta data, it becomes useful to search for files based on the Meta data contents. The Unix find utility was an early example, although inefficient when scanning hundreds of thousands of files on a modern computer system. Apple Computer's Mac OS X operating system supports cataloguing and searching for file Meta data through a feature known as Spotlight, as of version 10.4. Microsoft worked in the development of similar functionality with the Instant Search system in Windows Vista, as well as being present in SharePoint Server. Linux implements file Meta data using extended file attributes.

7. Image Meta Data

Examples of image files containing Meta data include

Exchangeable image file format (EXIF) and Tagged Image File Format (TIFF).

Having Meta data about images embedded in TIFF or EXIF files is one way of acquiring additional data about an image. Tagging pictures with subjects, related emotions, and other descriptive phrases helps Internet users find pictures easily rather than having to search through entire image collections. A prime example of an image tagging service is Flickr, where users upload images and then describe the contents. Other patrons of the site can then search for those tags. Flickr uses a folksonomy: a free-text keyword system in which the community defines the vocabulary through use rather than through a controlled vocabulary.

Users can also tag photos for organization purposes using Adobe's Extensible Meta data Platform (XMP) language, for example.

Digital photography is increasingly making use of technical Meta data tags describing the conditions of exposure. Photographers shooting Camera RAW file formats can use applications such as Adobe Bridge or Apple Computer's Aperture to work with camera Meta data for post-processing.

8. Program Meta Data

Meta data is casually used to describe the controlling data used in software architectures that are more abstract or configurable. Most **executable file** formats include what may be termed "meta data" that specifies certain, usually configurable, behavioral runtime characteristics. However, it is difficult if not impossible to precisely distinguish program "meta data" from general aspects of stored-program computing architecture; if the machine reads it and acts upon it, it is a computational instruction, and the prefix "meta" has little significance.

In Java, the class file format contains Meta data used by the Java compiler and the Java virtual machine to dynamically link classes and to support reflection. The J2SE 5.0 version of Java included a Meta data facility to allow additional annotations that are used by development tools.

In MS-DOS, the COM file format does *not* include meta data, while the EXE file and Windows PE formats do. These

Meta data can include the company that published the program, the date the program was created, the version number and more.

In the Microsoft .NET executable format, extra Meta data is included to allow reflection at runtime.

9. Existing Software Meta Data

Object Management Group (OMG) has defined Meta data format for representing entire existing applications for the purposes of software mining, software modernization and software assurance. This specification, called the OMG Knowledge Discovery Metamodel (KDM) is the OMG's foundation for "modeling in reverse". KDM is a common language-independent intermediate representation that provides an integrated view of an entire enterprise application, including its behavior (program flow), data, and structure. One of the applications of KDM is Business Rules Mining.

Knowledge Discovery Metamodel includes a fine grained low-level representation (called "micro KDM"), suitable for performing static analysis of programs.

10. Document Meta Data

Most programs that create documents, including Microsoft SharePoint, Microsoft Word and other Microsoft Office products, save Meta data with the document files. These Meta data can contain the name of the person who created the file (obtained from the operating system), the name of the person who last edited the file, how many times the file has been printed, and even how many revisions have been made on the file. Other saved material, such as deleted text (saved in case of an undelete command), document comments and the like, is also commonly referred to as "meta data", and the inadvertent inclusion of this material in distributed files has sometimes led to undesirable disclosures.

Document Meta data is particularly important in legal environments where litigation can request this sensitive information (meta data) which can include many elements of private detrimental data. This data has been linked to multiple lawsuits that have got corporations into legal complications.

Many legal firms today use "Meta data Management Software", also known as "Meta data Removal Tools". This software can be used to clean documents before they are sent outside of their firm. This process, known as Meta data management, protects lawfirms from potentially unsafe leaking of sensitive data through Electronic Discovery.

11. Meta Models

Meta data on Models are called Metamodels. In Model Driven Engineering, a Model has to conform to a given Metamodel. According to the MDA guide, a metamodel is a model and each model conforms to a given metamodel. Meta-modeling allows strict and agile automatic processing of models and metamodels. The Object Management Group (OMG) defines 4 layers of meta-modeling. Each level of modeling is defined, validated by the next layer:

- MO: instance object, data row, record -> "John Smith".
- Ml: model, schema -> "Customer" UML Class or database Table.
- M2: metamodel -> Unified Modeling Language (UML), Common Warehouse Metamodel (CWM), Knowledge Discovery Metamodel (KDM).
- M3: meta-metamodel -> Meta-Object Facility (MOF) Xegy uses meta data.

Meta Meta Data

Since Meta data are also data, it is possible to have Meta data of meta data—"meta-meta data." Machine-generated meta-meta data, such as the reversed index created by a free-text search engine, is generally not considered meta data, though.

12. Digital Library Meta Data

There are three categories of Meta data that are frequently used to describe objects in a digital library:

1. **Descriptive**—Information describing the intellectual content of the object, such as MARC cataloguing

records, finding aids or similar schemes. It is typically used for bibliographic purposes and for search and retrieval.

2. **Structural**—Information that ties each object to others to make up logical units (e.g., information that relates individual images of pages from a book to the others that make up the book).
3. **Administrative**—Information used to manage the object or control access to it. This may include information on how it was scanned, its storage format, copyright and licensing information, and information necessary for the long-term preservation of the digital objects.

13. Geospatial Meta Data

Meta data that describe geographic objects (such as datasets, maps, features, or simply documents with a geospatial component) have a history going back to at least 1994.

QUESTIONS

1. Explain the concept of meta data.
2. Define Meta data and Markup.
3. Differentiate data and meta data.
4. Describe various types of meta data.
5. Describe the use of meta data.
6. Identify the important issues of meta data.
7. Describe the classes of meta data.

11

Data Mining Structure

1. OBJECTIVES

- Understanding the concept of Data Mining
- To Know how Data Mining Obtained from the past
- Describe the Uses of Data Mining

2. WHAT IS DATA MINING?

Data mining is the process of sorting through large amounts of data and picking out relevant information. It is usually used by business intelligence organizations, and financial analysts, but is increasingly being used in the sciences to extract information from the enormous data sets generated by modern experimental and observational methods. It has been described as "the non-trivial extraction of implicit, previously unknown, and potentially useful information from data" and "the science of extracting useful information from large data sets or databases." Data mining in relation to enterprise resource planning is the statistical and logical analysis of large sets of transaction data, looking for patterns that can aid decision-making.

3. HISTORY OF DATA MINING

Traditionally, business analysts have performed the task of extracting useful information from recorded data, but the increasing volume of data in modern business and science calls for computer-based approaches. As data sets have grown in size and complexity, there has been a shift away from direct hands-on data analysis toward indirect, automatic data analysis using more complex and sophisticated tools. The modern technologies of computers, networks, and sensors have made data collection and organization much easier. However, the captured data needs to be converted into information and knowledge to become useful. Data mining is the entire process of applying computer-based methodology, including new techniques for knowledge discovery, to data

Data mining identifies trends within data that go beyond simple analysis. Through the use of sophisticated algorithms, non-statistician users have the opportunity to identify key attributes of business processes and target opportunities. However, abdicating control of this process from the statistician to the machine may result in false-positives or no useful results at **all.**

Although data mining is a relatively new term, the technology is not. For many years, businesses have used powerful computers to sift through volumes of data such as supermarket scanner data to produce market research reports (although reporting is not considered to be data mining). Continuous innovations in computer processing power, disk storage, and statistical software are dramatically increasing the accuracy and usefulness of data analysis.

The term data mining is often used to apply to the two separate processes of knowledge discovery and prediction. Knowledge discovery provides explicit information that has a readable form and can be understood by a user. Forecasting, or predictive modeling provides predictions of future events and may be transparent and readable/in some approaches (e.g., rule-based systems) and opaque in others such as neural networks. Moreover, some data-mining systems such as neural networks are inherently geared towards prediction and pattern recognition, rather than knowledge discovery.

Metadata, or data about a given data set, are often expressed in a condensed *data-minable* format, or one that facilitates the practice of data mining. Common examples include executive summaries and scientific abstracts.

Data mining relies on the use of real world data. This data is extremely vulnerable to collinearity precisely because data from the real world may have unknown interrelations. An unavoidable weakness of data mining is that the critical data that may expose any relationship might have never been observed. Alternative approaches using an experiment-based approach such as Choice Modelling for human-generated data may be used. Inherent correlations are either controlled for or removed altogether through the construction of an experimental design.

Recently, there were some efforts to define a standard for data mining, for example, the CRISP-DM standard for analysis processes or the Java Data-Mining Standard. Independent of these standardization efforts, freely available open-source software systems like RapidMiner and Weka have become an informal standard for defining data-mining processes.

There are also privacy and human rights concerns associated with data mining, specifically regarding the source of the data analyzed. Data mining provides information that may be difficult to obtain otherwise. When the data collected involves individual people, there are many questions concerning privacy, legality, and ethics. In particular, data mining government or commercial data sets for national security or law enforcement purposes has raised privacy concerns.'

4. USES OF DATA MINING

1. Games

Since the early 1960s, with the availability of oracles for certain combinatorial games, also called tablebases (e.g. for 3x3-chess) with any beginning configuration, small-board dots-and-boxes, small-board-hex, and certain endgames in chess, dots-and-boxes, and hex; a new area for data mining has been opened up. This is the extraction of human-usable strategies from these oracles. Current pattern recognition approaches do not seem to fully have the required high level of abstraction in order to be applied successfully. Instead, extensive experimentation with the tablebases, combined with an intensive study of tablebase-answers to well designed problems and with knowledge of prior art, i.e. pre-tablebase knowledge, is used to yield insightful patterns. Berlekamp in dots-and-boxes etc. and John Nunn in chess endgames are notable examples of researchers doing this work, though they were not and are not involved in tablebase generation.

2. Business

Data mining in customer relationship management applications can contribute significantly to the bottom *line.* Rather than contacting a prospect or customer through a call center or sending mail, only prospects that are predicted to have a high likelihood of responding to an offer are contacted. More sophisticated methods may be used to optimize across campaigns so that we can predict which channel and which offer an individual is most likely to respond to across all potential offers. Finally, in cases where many people will take an action without an offer, uplift modeling can be used to determine which people will have the greatest increase in responding if given an offer. Data clustering can also be used to automatically discover the segments or groups within a customer data set.

Businesses employing data mining quickly see a return on investment, but also they recognize that the number of predictive models can quickly become very large. Rather than one model to predict which customers will churn, a business could build a separate model for each region and customer type. Then instead of sending an offer to all people that are likely to churn, it may only want to send offers to customers that will likely take to offer. And finally, it may also want to determine which customers are going to be profitable over a window of time and only send the offers to those that are likely to be profitable. In order to maintain this quantity of models, they need to manage model versions and move to *automated data mining.*

Data mining can also be helpful to human-resources departments in identifying the characteristics of their most successful employees. Information obtained, such as universities attended by highly successful employees, can help HR focus recruiting efforts accordingly. Additionally, Strategic Enterprise Management applications help a company translate corporate-level goals, such as profit and margin share targets, into operational decisions, such as production plans and workforce levels.

Another example of data mining, often called the market basket analysis, relates to its use in retail sales. If a clothing store records the purchases of customers, a data-mining system could identify those customers who favour silk shirts over cotton ones. Although some explanations of relationships may be difficult, taking advantage of it is easier. The example deals with association rules within transaction-based data. Not all data are transaction-based and logical or inexact rules may also be present within a database.

Related to an integrated-circuit production line, an example of data mining is described in the paper "Mining IC Test Data to Optimize VLSI Testing." In this paper the application of data mining and decision analysis to the problem of die-level functional test is described. Experiments mentioned in this paper demonstrate the ability of applying a system of mining historical die-test data to create a probabilistic model of patterns of die failure which are then utilized to decide in real time which die to test next and when to stop testing. This system has been shown, based on experiments with historical test data, to have the potential to improve profits on mature IC products.

3. Science and Engineering

In recent years, data mining has been widely used in area of science and engineering, such as bioinformatics, genetics, medicine, education, and electrical power engineering.

In the area of study on human genetics, the important goal is to understand the mapping relationship between the inter-individual variation in human DNA sequences and variability in disease susceptibility. In lay terms, it is to find out how the changes in an individual's DNA sequence affect the risk of developing common diseases such as cancer. This is very important to help improve the diagnosis, prevention and treatment of the diseases. The data mining technique that is used to perform this task is known as multifactor dimensionality reduction.

In the area of electrical power engineering, data mining techniques have been widely used for condition monitoring of high voltage electrical equipment. The purpose of condition monitoring is to obtain valuable information on the insulation's health status of the equipment. Data clustering such as self-organizing map (SOM) has been applied on the vibration monitoring and analysis of transformer on-load tap-changers (OLTCS). Using vibration monitoring, it can be observed that each tap change operation generates a signal that contains information about the condition of the tap changer contacts and the drive mechanisms. Obviously, different tap positions will generate different signals. However, there was considerable variability amongst normal condition signals for the exact same tap position. SOM has been applied to detect abnormal conditions and to estimate the nature of the abnormalities.

Data mining techniques have also been applied for dissolved gas analysis (DGA) on power transformers. DGA, as a diagnostics for power transformer, has been available for centuries. Data mining techniques such as SOM has been applied to analyse data and to determine trends which are not obvious to the standard DGA ratio techniques such as Duval Triangle.

A fourth area of application for data mining in science/ engineering is within educational research, where data mining has been used to study the factors leading students to choose to engage in behaviors which reduce their learning and to understand the factors influencing university student retention.

Other examples or applying data mining technique applications are biomedical data facilitated by domain ontologies mining clinical trial data, traffic analysis using SOM, et cetera.

4. Combatting Terrorism

Data mining has been cited as the method by which the U.S. Army unit Able Danger had identified the September 11, 2001 attacks leader, Mohamed Atta, and three other 9/11 hijackers as possible members of an Al Qaeda cell operating in the U.S. more than a year before the attack.

It has been suggested that both the Central Intelligence Agency and the Canadian Security Intelligence Service have employed this method.

Previous data mining to stop terrorist programs under the US government include the Terrorism Information Awareness (TIA) program, Computer-Assisted Passenger Prescreening System (CAPPS II), Analysis, Dissemination, Visualization, Insight, and Semantic Enhancement (ADVISE), Multlstate Antl-Terrorism Information Exchange (MATRIX), and the Secure Flight program Security—MSNBC. These programs have been discontinued due to controversy over whether they violate the US Constitution's 4th amendment.

QUESTIONS

1. Explain the concept of Data Mining.
2. Describe how the Data Mining had Obtained from the past.
3. Describe the Uses of Data Mining.

12

Text Mining

1. OBJECTIVES

- Understanding the concept of Text Mining
- To Know how Text Mining Obtained from the past
- Describe the Applications of Text Mining
- Describe the Implications of Text Mining

2. WHAT IS TEXT MINING?

Text mining, sometimes alternately referred to as *text data mining,* refers generally to the process of deriving high quality information from text. High quality information is typically derived through the dividing of patterns and trends through means such as statistical pattern learning. Text mining usually involves the process of structuring the input text (usually parsing, along with the addition of some derived linguistic features and the removal of others, and subsequent insertion into a database), deriving patterns within the structured data, and finally evaluation and interpretation of the output. 'High quality' in text mining usually refers to some combination of relevance, novelty, and interestingness. Typical text mining tasks include text categorization, text clustering, concept/entity extraction, production of granular taxonomies, sentiment analysis, document summarization, and entity relation modeling (i.e., learning relations between named entities).

3. HISTORY OF TEXT MINING

Labour-intensive manual text-mining approaches first surfaced in the mid-1980s, but technological advances have enabled the field to advance swiftly during the past decade. Text mining is an interdisciplinary field which draws on information retrieval, data mining, machine learning, statistics, and computational linguistics. As most information (over 80%) is currently stored as text, text mining is believed to have a high commercial potential value. Increasing interest is being paid to multilingual data mining: the ability to gain information across languages and cluster similar items from different linguistic sources according to their meaning.

Sentiment Analysis

Sentiment analysis may, for example, involve analysis of movie reviews for estimating how favorably a review is for a movie. Such an analysis may require a labeled data set or labeling of the affectiveness of words. A resource for affectiveness of words have been made for WordNetJ.

4. APPLICATIONS IN TEXT MINING

Recently, text mining has been receiving attention in many areas.

1. Security Applications

One of the largest text mining applications that exists is probably the classified ECHELON surveillance system. Additionally, many text mining software packages such as AeroText, Attensity, SPSS and Expert System are marketed towards security applications, particularly analysis of plain text sources such as Internet news.

In 2007, Europol's Serious Crime division developed an analysis system in order to track transnational organized crime. This Overall Analysis System for Intelligence Support (OASIS) integrates among the most advanced text analytics and text mining technologies available on today's market. This system led Europol to make the most significant progress to support law enforcement objectives at the international level.

2. Biomedical Applications

A range of applications of text mining of the biomedical literature has been described. One example is PubGene (pubgene.org) that combines biomedical text mining with network visualization as an Internet service. Another example, which uses ontologies with textmining is GoPubMed.org.

3. Marketing Applications

Text mining is starting to be used in marketing as well, more specifically in analytical Customer relationship management. Coussement and Van den Poel (2008) apply it to improve predictive analytics models for customer churn (Customer attrition).

4. Academic Applications

The issue of text mining is of importance to publishers who hold large databases of information requiring indexing for retrieval. This is particularly true in scientific disciplines, in which highly specific information is often contained within written text. Therefore, initiatives have been taken such as Nature's proposal for an Open Text Mining publisher barriers to public access.

Academic institutions have also become involved in the text mining initiative:

> The National Centre for Text Mining, a collaborative effort between the Universities of Manchester and Liverpool, provides customised tools, research facilities and offers advice to the academic community. They are funded by the Joint Information Systems Committee (JISC) and two of the UK Research Councils. With an initial focus on text mining in the biological and biomedical sciences, research has since expanded into the areas of Social Science.

In the United States, the School of Information at University of California, Berkeley is developing a program called BioText to assist bioscience researchers in text mining and analysis.

5. Software and Applications

Research and development departments of major companies, including IBM and Microsoft, are researching text mining techniques and developing programs to further automate the mining and analysis processes. Text mining software is also being researched by different companies working in the area of search and indexing in general as a way to improve their results. There is a large number of companies that provide commercial computer programs:

- AeroText—provides a suite of text mining applications for content analysis. Content used can be in multiple languages.
- Attensity—suite of text mining solutions that includes search, statistical and NLP-based technologies for a" variety of industries.
- Autonomy—suite of text mining, clustering and categorization solutions for a variety of industries.
- Endeca Technologies—provides software to analyze and cluster unstructured text.
- Expert System S.p.A.—suite of semantic technologies and products for developers and knowledge managers.
- Fair Isaac—leading provider of decision management solutions powered by advanced analytics (includes text analytics).
- Language Ware—the IBM Tools and Runtime for Text Mining.
- Inxight—provider of text analytics, search, and unstructured visualization technologies. (Inxight was sold to Business Objects that was sold to SAP AG in 2007).
- Nstein Technologies [2]--provider of text mining, digital asset management and web content management solutions.

- Pervasive Data Integrator—includes Extract Schema Designer that allows the user to point and click identify structure patterns in reports, html, emails, etc. for extraction into any database
- RapidMiner/YALE—open-source data and text mining software for scientific and commercial use.
- SPSS—provider of SPSS Text Analysis for Surveys, Text Mining for Clementine, LexiQuest Mine and LexiQuest Categorize, commercial text analytics software that can be used in conjunction with SPSS Predictive Analytics Solutions.
- Thomson Data Analyzer—Enables complex analysis on patent information, scientific publications and news.
- Clearforest Developer—A suite of tools for developing NLP (Natural Language Processing)-based text mining applications to derive structure out of unstructured texts.
- VantagePoint [3]—Text mining software which includes tools for data cleanup, analysis, process automation, and reporting.

Open-source Software and Applications

- GATE—natural language processing and language engineering tool.
- YALE/RapidMiner with its Word Vector Tool plugin-data and text mining software.
- tm [4] [5]—text mining in the R programming language

5. IMPLICATIONS

Until recently websites most often used text-based lexical searches; in other words, users could find documents only by the words that happened to occur in the documents. Text mining may allow searches to be directly answered by the semantic web; users may be able to search for content based on its meaning and context, rather than just by a specific word.

Additionally, text mining software can be used to build large dossiers of information about specific people and events. For example, by using software that extracts specifics facts about businesses and individuals from news reports, large datasets can be built to facilitate social networks analysis or counter-intelligence. In effect, the text mining software may act in a capacity similar to an intelligence analyst or research librarian, albeit with a more limited scope of analysis.

Text mining is also used in some email spam filters as a way of determining the characteristics of messages that are likely to be advertisements or other unwanted material.

- Ronen Feldman and James Sanger, *The Text Mining Handbook,* Cambridge University Press, ISBN 9780521836579.
- Kao Anne, Poteet, Steve R. (Editors), Natural Language Processing and Text Mining, Springer, ISBN-10: 184628175X.
- Konchady Manu "Text Mining Application Programming (Programming Series)" by Manu Konchady, Charles River Media, ISBN 1584504609.
- M. Ikonomakis, S. Kotsiantis, V. Tampakas, Text Classification Using Machine Learning Techniques, WSEAS Transactions on Computers, Issue 8, Volume 4, August 2005, pp. 966-974 (http://www.math.upatras.gr/~esdlab/en/members/kotsiantis/Text%20Classification% 20final%20journal.pdf).

QUESTIONS

1. Describe the concept of Text Mining.
2. Write the history of Text Mining.
3. Describe the Applications of Text Mining.
4. Describe the Implications of Text Mining.

13

Semantic Web

1. OBJECTIVES

- Understanding the concept of Semantic Web
- Describe the need for semantic Web
- Describe various Components of Semantic Web
- Discuss the various projects in Semantic Web
- Identify the various services in Semantic Web

2. INTRODUCTION

The **Semantic Web** is an evolving extension of the World Wide Web in which the semantics of information and services on the web is defined, making it possible for the web to understand and satisfy the requests of people and machines to use the web content. It derives from W3C director Tim Berners-Lee's vision of the Web as a universal medium for data, information, and knowledge exchange.

At its core, the semantic web comprises a set of design principles, collaborative working groups, and a variety of enabling technologies. Some elements of the semantic web are expressed as prospective future possibilities that are yet to be implemented or realized. Other elements of the semantic web are expressed in formal specifications. Some of these include Resource Description Framework (RDF), a variety of data interchange formats (e.g. RDF/XML, N3, Turtle, N-Triples), and notations such as RDF Schema (RDFS) and the Web Ontology Language (OWL), all of which are intended to provide a formal description of concepts, terms, and relationships within a given knowledge domain.

3. NEED FOR SEMANTIC WEB

Humans are capable of using the Web to carry out tasks such as finding the Finnish word for "cat", reserving a library book, and searching for a low price on a DVD. However, a computer cannot accomplish the same tasks without human direction because web pages are designed to be read by people, not machines. The semantic web is a vision of information that is understandable by computers, so that they can perform more of the tedious work involved in finding, sharing and combining information on the web.

Tim Berners-Lee originally expressed the vision of the semantic web as follows:

> *have a dream for the Web [in which computers] become capable of analyzing all the data on the Web—the content, links, and transactions between people and computers. A 'Semantic Web', which should make this possible, has yet to emerge, but when it does, the day-to-day mechanisms of trade, bureaucracy and our daily lives will be handled by machines talking to machines. The 'intelligent agents' people have touted for ages will finally materialize.*

Semantic publishing will benefit greatly from the semantic web. In particular, the semantic web is expected to revolutionize scientific publishing, such as real-time publishing and sharing of experimental data on the Internet. This simple but radical idea is now being explored by W3C HCLS group's Scientific Publishing Task Force.

Tim Berners-Lee has further stated:

People keep asking 'what Web 3.0 is' I think maybe when you've got an overlay of scalable vector graphics—everything rippling and folding and looking misty—on Web 2.0 and access to a semantic Web integrated across a huge space of data, you'll have access to an unbelievable data resource.

4. RELATIONSHIP TO THE HYPERTEXT WEB

1. Markup

Many files on a typical computer can be loosely divided into documents and data. Documents like mail messages, reports, and brochures are read by humans. Data, like calendars, addressbooks, playlists, and spreadsheets are presented using an application program which lets them be viewed, searched and combined in many ways.

Currently, the World Wide Web is based mainly on documents written in Hypertext Markup Language (HTML), a markup convention that is used for coding a body of text interspersed with multimedia objects such as images and interactive forms. Metadata tags, for example

<meta name^'keywords" content="computing, computer studies, computer"> <meta name="description" content=" Cheap widgets for sale"> <meta name="author" content="Hack's Hardware">

provide a method by which computers can categorise the content of web pages.

The semantic web takes the concept further; it involves publishing the data in a language, Resource Description Framework (RDF), specifically for data, so that it can be categorized as human perception and be "understood" by computers. So all data is not only stored, but filed and well handled.

HTML describes documents and the links between them. RDF, by contrast, describes arbitrary things such as people, meetings, or airplane parts.

For example, with HTML and a tool to render it (perhaps Web browser software, perhaps another user agent), one can create and present a page that lists items for sale. The HTML of this catalog page can make simple, document-level assertions such as "this document's title is 'Widget Superstore". But there is no capability within the HTML itself to assert unambiguously that, for example, item number X586172 is an Acme Gizmo with a retail price of €199, or that it is a consumer product. Rather, HTML can only say that the span of text "X586172" is something that should be positioned near "Acme Gizmo" and "€ 199", etc. There is no way to say "this is a catalog" or even to establish that "Acme Gizmo" is a kind of title or that "€ 199" is a price. There is also no way to express that these pieces of information are bound together in describing a discrete item, distinct from other items perhaps listed on the page.

2. Descriptive and Extensible

The semantic web addresses this shortcoming, using the descriptive technologies Resource Description Framework (RDF) and Web Ontology Language (OWL), and the data-centric, customizable Extensible Markup Language (XML). These technologies are combined in order to provide descriptions that supplement or replace the content of Web documents. Thus, content may manifest as descriptive data stored ' in Web-accessible databases, or as markup within documents (particularly, in Extensible HTML (XHTML) interspersed with XML, or, more often, purely in XML, with layout/rendering cues stored separately). The machine-readable descriptions enable content managers to add meaning to the content, i.e. to *describe the structure of the knowledge we have about that content. In* this way, a machine can process knowledge itself, instead of text, using processes similar to human deductive reasoning and inference, thereby obtaining more meaningful results and facilitating automated information gathering and research by computers.

3. Semantic *vs.* non-Semantic Web

Example tags that would be used in Non-semantic web page

<item>cat</item>

A tag that would be used by Semantic web 'page': <item rdf:about="http://dbpedia.org/resource/Cat">Cat</item>

4. Practical Feasibility

Critics question the basic feasibility of a complete or even partial fulfilment of the semantic web. Some develop their critique from the perspective of human behavior and personal preferences, which ostensibly diminish the likelihood of its fulfilment. Other commentators object that there are limitations that stem from the current state of software engineering itself.

Where semantic web technologies have found a greater degree of practical adoption, it has tended to be among core specialized communities and organizations for intra-company projects. The practical constraints toward adoption have appeared less challenging where domain and scope is more limited than that of the general public and the World-Wide Web.

5. An Unrealized Idea

The original 2001 Scientific American article by Berners-Lee described an expected evolution of the existing Web to a Semantic Web.Such an evolution has machine can process knowledge itself, instead of text, using processes similar to human deductive reasoning and inference, thereby obtaining more meaningful results and facilitating automated information gathering and research by computers.

6. Censorship and Privacy

Enthusiasm about the semantic web could be tempered by concerns regarding censorship and privacy. For instance, text-analyzing techniques can now be easily bypassed by using other words, metaphors for instance, or by using images in place of words. An advanced implementation of the semantic web would make it much easier for governments to control the viewing and creation of online information, as this information would be much easier for an automated content-blocking machine to understand. In addition, the issue has also been raised that, with the use of FOAF files and geo location metadata, there would be very little anonymity associated with the authorship of articles on things such as a personal blog.

7. Doubling Output Formats

Another criticism of the semantic web is that it would be much more time-consuming to create and publish content because there would need to be two formats for one piece of data: one for human viewing and one for machines. However, many web applications in development are addressing this issue by creating a machine-readable format upon the publishing of data or the request of a machine for such data. The development of microformats has been one reaction to this kind of criticism.

Specifications such as eRDF and RDFa allow arbitrary RDF data to be embedded in HTML pages. The GRDDL (Gleaning Resource Descriptions from Dralects of Language) mechanism allows existing material (including microformats) to be automatically interpreted as RDF, so publishers only need to use a single format, such as HTML.

The idea of a 'semantic web' necessarily coming from some marking code other than simple HTML is built on the assumption that it is not possible for a machine to appropriately interpret code based on nothing but the order relationships of letters and words. If this is not true, then a 'semantic web' may be possible built on HTML alone, making a specially built 'semantic web' coding system unnecessary.

There are latent dynamic network models that can, under certain conditions, be 'trained' to appropriately 'learn' meaning based on order data, in the process 'learning' relationships with order (a kind of rudimentary working grammar). See for example latent semantic analysis

5. COMPONENTS OF SEMANTIC WEB

The semantic web comprises the standards and tools of XML, XML Schema, RDF, RDF Schema and OWL that are organized in the Semantic Web Stack. The OWL Web Ontology

Language Overview describes the function and relationship of each of these components of the semantic web:

- XML provides an elemental syntax for content structure within documents, yet associates no semantics with the meaning of the content contained within.
- XML Schema is a language for providing and restricting the structure and content of elements contained within XML documents.
- RDF is a simple language for expressing data models, which refer to objects ("resources") and their relationships. An RDF-based model can be represented in XML syntax.
- RDF Schema is a vocabulary for describing properties and classes of RDF-based resources, with semantics for generalized-hierarchies of such properties and classes.
- OWL adds more vocabulary for describing properties and classes: among others, relations between classes (e.g. disjointness), cardinality (e.g. "exactly one"), equality, richer typing of properties, characteristics of properties (e.g. symmetry), and enumerated classes.
- SPARQL is a protocol and query language for semantic web data sources.

Current ongoing standardizations include:

- Rule Inter change P ormat (RIF) as the Rule Layer of the Semantic Web Stack

The intent is to enhance the usability and usefulness of the Web and its interconnected resources through:

- Servers which expose existing data systems using the RDF and SPARQL standards. Many converters to RDF exist from different applications. Relational databases are an important source. The semantic web server attaches to the existing system without affecting its operation.

- Documents "markedup" with semantic information (an extension of theHTML <meta> tags used in today's Web pages to supply information for Web search engines using web crawlers). This could be machine-understandable information about the human-understandable content of the document (such as the creator, title, description, etc., of the document) or it could be purely metadata representing a set of facts (such as resources and services elsewhere in the site). Semantic markup is often generated automatically, rather than manually.
- Common metadata vocabularies (ontologies) and maps between vocabularies that allow document creators to know how to markup their documents so that agents can use the information in the supplied metadata (so that *Author* in the sense of 'the Author of the page' won't be confused with *Author* in the sense of a book that is the subject of a book review).
- Automated agents to perform tasks for users of the semantic web using this data.
- Web-based services (often with agents of their own) to supply information specifically to agents (for example, a Trust service that an agent could ask if some online store has a history of poor service or spamming).

6. PROJECTS

Projects and tools, but is very incomplete. The choice of projects is somewhat arbitrary but may serve illustrative purposes.

1. Neurocommons

The Neurocommons is an open RDF database developed by Science Commons. It was compiled from major life sciences databases with a focus on neuroscience. It is accessible via a web-based front end using the SPARQL query language.

2. FOAF

A popular application of the semantic web is Friend of a

Friend (or FoaF), which describes relationships among people and other agents in terms of RDF.

3. SIOC

The SIOC Project—Semantically-Interlinked Online Communities provides a vocabulary of terms and relationships that model web data spaces. Examples of such data spaces include, among others: discussion forums, weblogs, blogrolls / feed subscriptions, mailing lists, shared bookmarks, image galleries.

4. SIMILE

Semantic Interoperability of Metadata and Information in unLike Environments Massachusetts Institute of Technology.

SIMILE is a joint project, conducted by the MIT Libraries and MIT CSAIL, which seeks to enhance interoperability among digital assets, schemata/vocabularies/ontologies, meta data, and services.

5. Linking Open Data

The Linking Open Data project is a community lead effort to create openly accessible, and interlinked, RDF Data on the Web. The data in question takes the form of RDF Data Sets drawn from a broad collection of data sources. There is a focus on the Linked Data style of publishing RDF on the Web. Web application as Linked Data.

The project is one of several sponsored by the W3C's Semantic Web Education & Outreach Interest Group (SWEO).

7. SERVICES

1. Notification Services

Semantic Web Ping Service

The Semantic Web Ping Service is a notification service for the semantic web that tracks the creation and modification of RDF-based data sources on the Web. It provides Web Services for loosely coupled monitoring of RDF data. In addition, it provides a breakdown of RDF data sources tracked by vocabulary that includes: SIOC, FOAF, DOAP, RDFS, and OWL.

Piggy Bank

Another freely downloadable tool is the Piggy Bank plug-into firefox. Piggy Bank works by extracting or translating web scripts into RDF information and storing this information on the user's computer. This information can then be retrieved independently of the original context and used in other contexts, for example by using Google Maps to display information. Piggy Bank works with a new service, Semantic Bank, which combines the idea of tagging information with the new web languages. Piggy Bank was developed by the Simile Project, which also provides RDFizers, tools that can be used to translate specific types of information, for example weather reports for US zip codes, into RDF. Efforts like these could ease a potentially troublesome transition between the web of today and its semantic successor.

Triplify

Triplify is a small plugin for database driven Web applications which:

- exposes RDF, Linked Data and JSON,
- is extremely simple to configure—just provide some SQL queries, selecting the information to be exposed,
- is complemented by a light-weight registry for RDF data sources.

Since the Web mainly consists of Web pages served by a relatively small number of Web applications (consider all the Drupal, Wordpress and MediaWiki installations) once a Triplify configuration is created it can be reused without modifications for other instances of the same Web application thus making the Web applications very easy.

Pags Databases

Webepags Databases is an application that allows users to create an rdf database in the browser, without any knowledge necessary.

- Antoniou, Grigoris (2004-04-01), *A Semantic Web Primer.* The MIT Press. ISBN 0262012103.
- Davies, John (2006-07-11). *Semantic Web Technologies: Trends and Research in Ontology-based Systems,* Wiley, ISBN 0470025964.
- Passin, Thomas B. (2004-03-01), *Explorer's Guide to the Semantic Web,* Manning Publications, ISBN 1932394206.

QUESTIONS

1. Write the various concept of Semantic web.
2. Describe the need for semantic web.
3. What are the various Components of Semantic Web?
4. Write the various projects in Semantic Web?
5. What are the various services available in Semantic Web?

PART V

Digital Library

14

Basic Concepts of Digital Library Structure

1. OBJECTIVES

- Understanding the concept of Digital Library
- Different Digital Library Functions
- Describe Various Functions of Digital Library
- Identify the Advantages of Digital Library

2. INTRODUCTION

Libraries are of different types and exist in many forms such as traditional library, electronic library, digital library, virtual library, hybrid library, etc. The advent of multimedia technology has given rise to image libraries, Audio libraries, and Digital libraries.

3. WHAT IS DIGITAL LIBRARY?

Digital library is a library that contains material in a digitalised form. It can also be defined as the library that contains digital material. The digital library has materials stored in a computer system in a form that allows it to be manipulated and delivered in ways that the conventional version of the material cannot be.

4. DEFINITION FOR DIGITAL LIBRARY

According to Lesk a digital library is "a collection of information that is both digitized and organized and which offers capabilities beyond those of the traditional library".

Larson defines a digital library as a "global virtual library—the library of thousands of networked electronic libraries".

The workshop entitled "Interoperability, Scaling and Digital Library Research Agenda" defined a digital library as "An organized collection of multimedia data with information management methods that represent the data as information and knowledge".

Digital library is "an organized collection of multimedia data with information management methods that represent the data as useful information and knowledge to people in a variety of social and organizational contexts" says Griffin, "The concept of digital libraries is not merely equivalent to a digitized collection with information management tools. It is rather an environment to bring together collections, services and people in support of the full life cycle of creation, dissemination, use and preservation of data, information and knowledge.

There are many definitions of a "digital library". Terms such as "Electronic library" and "virtual library" are often used synonymously. The elements that have been identified as common to these definitions are:

- The digital library is not a single entity;
- The digital library requires technology to iink the resources of many;
- The linkages between the many digital libraries and information services are transparent to the end users:
- Universal access to digital libraries and information services is a goal of many digital libraries.

- Digital library collections are limited to document surrogates: They extend to digital artifacts that cannot be represented or distributed in printed formats.
- To gain knowledge what constitutes digital library let us have a look into a few definitions of digital library.
- A digital library is, "a managed environment of multimedia materials in digital form, designed for the benefit of its user population, structured to facilitate access to its contents, and equipped with aids to navigate the global network . . . with users and holdings totally distributed, but managed as acoherent whole." Mel Collier.
- Sun Microsystems defines a digital library as the elecrronic extension of functions users typically perform and the resources they access in a traditional library. The information resources for a digital library can be translated into digital form, stored in multimedia repositories, and made available through Web-based services.

In general, the digital library is a structured, processed and organized digital repository of knowledge. Such a repository is created to serve the user community as the traditional library.

5. DIGITAL LIBRARY DEVELOPMENT—ISSUES

A digital library is not confined to just digitized collection. It should be built according to principles that are not necessarily the same as those employed for paper collections, and it should be evaluated according to different measures that are no yet totally clear and not defined perfectly.

1. Digital Conversion Process

Digital conversion process includes :

- Document

- Data Capture
- Data Processing
- Storage
- Indexing and Processing
- Retrieval and display.

Documents—It include text, bibliographic or full text, Photographs, diagrams, charts, maps, colour images, etc. They exist either in print or non-print form and also as single unit or collections.

Data Capture—It includes manual data entry (word processing), optical character recognition (OCR) or imaging using scanners.

Data processing—The text in the convertible document may require conversion of diacritics or special characters: images may need enhancement, amplification or compression. In many cases a simple conversion from print to digital is not enough.

Storage—The digitized information needs to be recorded in proper digital storage medium, which may be hard disk, magnetic tape, optical CD-ROM, or networks with workstation to access.

Indexing and Processing—Digitised documents need to be processed using standards, protocols and indexing systems. Classification using library systems also hold much promise. Metadata application should be a major component of the digital information processing.

Retrieval/Display—It is the process through which an array of technologies browsing, displaying, and applying packages that ultimately helps in access.

Digitalization also involves the addition of new digital collection to the existing one with proper interface.

6. FUNCTIONS OF DIGITAL LIBRARY

The function of digital library is to create, maintain, manage, access to and preservation of digital contents. The information repositories are created by producing the information content in digital form or converting the print to digital form, stored in multimedia repositories, and made available through intranet or internet or from any server to the workstations.

The major functional components of a digital library are:

- Conversion of print to digital and acquisition of digital media;
- Metadata creation, processing and description;
- Storing of digital resource in appropriate repository in a networked environment for hosting in intranet, extranet and internet;
- Creating a single user interface and gateway for the digital resources; and
- Patron access through a browser or dedicated client.

The above components are mandatory for all digital delivery system nor these alone do not constitute a well-designed digital library. An ideal digital library has to work in conjunction with or without creating a parallel information delivery mechanism. The major requisite is the interoperability and interface with the existing collection. This is a much complex process and there is no consistent and uniform way is evolved for doing it.

7. ADVANTAGES OF DIGITAL LIBRARIES

With digital libraries, an individual can:

- Gain access to the holdings of libraries worldwide through automated catalogues.
- Locate both physical and digitized versions of scholarly articles and books.
- Optimize searches, simultaneously search the Internet, commercial databases, and library collections.
- Save search results and conduct additional processing to narrow or qualify results.
- From search results, click through to access the digitized content or locate additional items of interest.

8. CONCLUSION

Digital libraries are distinguished from information retrieval systems because they include more types of media, provide additional functionality and services, and include other stages of the information life cycle, from creation through use. Digital libraries can be viewed as a new form of information institution or as an extension of the services libraries currently provided.

Growth in web-accessible resources and development in related technologies such as digital libraries have opened up exciting new possibilities for document access. Advances in computing power and steep reduction in computing cost have spurred renewed interest in application of artificial intelligence techniques in document access.

QUESTIONS

1. Define the concept of Digital Library.
2. Write the Digital Library functions.
3. Describe various issues of Digital Library.
4. Define the advantages of Digital Library.

15

Principles of Digitization

1. OBJECTIVES

- Understanding the concept of Digitization
- Need for Digitization
- Describe various Digitization Techniques
- Different types of Digitization
- Describe the trends in Digitization
- Identify the various issues in Digitization

2. WHAT IS DIGITIZATION?

Cornell University Library defines digital images as: "electronic snapshots taken of a scene of scanned from documents, such as photographs, manuscripts, printed texts, and artwork. The digital image is sampled and mapped as a grid of dots or picture elements (pixels). Each pixel is assigned a tonal value (black, white, shades of gray or color), which is represented in binary code (zeros and ones). The binary digits ("bits) for each pixel are stored in a sequence by a computer and often reduced to a mathematical representation (compressed). The bits are then interpreted and read by the computer to produce an analog version for display or printing."

> In brief, digitization converts materials from formats that can be read by people (analog) to a format that can be read only by machines (digital). Flatbed scanning, digital cameras, planetary cameras, and a number of other devices can be used to digitize cultural heritage materials.

3. SELECTION OF DIGITIZATION

Selection of digitization is a complicated process. Decisions about what to digitize must first and foremost address the intellectual value of the original sources. Conversion of textual, visual and numeric information to electronic form, however, involves additional layers of complexity. The digitization process, from preparation and conversion to presentation and archiving encompasses a range of procedures and technologies with widely varying implications and costs. Digital reformatting of library collections is still in its infancy, at once limiting what can be accomplished now and forcing decision-makers to anticipate future improvements.

Materials with marginal scholarly value are best left in their original form or made accessible in a less costly manner. Scholarly value, of course, is a subjective assessment and even most marginal materials can support some kinds of research. Most users, nonetheless, opt for electronic access to original monographs rather than to derivative works.

4. CONCEPT OF DIGITIZATION

The term "digitization" refers to the electronic process of converting a document in a non-digital medium into digital form for storage, retrieval and transmission. Digitization is defined as the process of transferring print media into a computer-readable format, and organizing and presenting that data in a way that is useful to users. Another explanatory definition of digitization is "the process of translating a piece of information such as a book, sound recording, picture or video, into bits". The digitization process can be accomplished through a variety of existing technologies, and may comprise any or all of the following steps:

- Creation
- Dissemination
- Organization

Process Steps

Creation: The making of digital copies of analogue objects or the modification of original digital objects for purposes of digitization,

Dissemination: The provision of mechanisms by which the target population of users can gain access to the digitized material in the collection; and

Organization: The provision of search tools and finding aids for the user to access the collection of digitized or conventional objects effectively.

Conversion Process

- Document
  - Data Capture
    - Storage
      - Indexing and Processing
        - Retrieval and display

Digitization is presumed to add value to physical collections because:

- Digital content can lead to new knowledge by enabling scholarly use that was not possible with print collections—such as new forms of textual analysis and new forms of scholarly communication.
- The creation of new finding aids, links to bibliographic records, and development of metadata will enhance intellectual control of collections.
- Ability to search, discover, and manipulate images,

text, and sound in newcontexts will increase and extend use of collections.

- Wider dissemination of unique collections will encourage scholarly use.
- Digital surrogates will help preserve unique objects by protecting them from handling %.
- Digitization will allow integration of related materials on multiple hosts in "virtual collections".

5. WHY DIGITIZE?

It is often said that digital information is transforming the way we learn, the way we communicate, even the way we think. It is also changing the way that libraries and archives not only work, but more fundamentally, the very work that they do. It is early to overstate-and-underestimate—the transformative power of a new technology, especially when we do not yet understand the full implications of its many applications. Librarians everywhere hear the voices of people speaking enthusiastically, urging the conversion of text and visual materials into digital form as if conversion were a self-evident good.

While we may not yet fully understand the ways in which this technology will and will not change libraries, we can already discern some simple, yet profoundly important, patterns in digital applications that presage their effective and creative use the traditional library functions of collecting, preserving, and making information accessible. Digitization helps to preserve precious materials and to reduce wear and tear on fragile items. This does not mean however, that digital copies should be seen as a replacement for the original documents. Even after digitization, original documents and artifacts must still be cared.

6. DIGITIZATION TECHNIQUES

Original books, manuscripts, photographs or paintings, however are promising a resource, might be nearly unapproachable because of its size and the condition and dimensions of individual items. Some resources are too fragile to be consulted. Aging newspapers or palm-leaf manuscripts that break at the slightest flex simply cannot be browsed manually.

A person reading a book, looking at a photograph or consulting a manuscript encounters few barriers to use. One might have to handle an object carefully, or use a magnifying glass to read fine print, but in general the work is immediately approachable. The same resources, when digitized, should be equally accessible and approachable. Different digitizing techniques result in electronic files with different characteristics. The simplest approach to digitizing involves use of a scanner or digital camera to create electronic pictures of original materials. Scanning rare and unique texts or visual resources can make them accessible to users who would otherwise never see them. In such a case, merely reproducing the original in electronic form represents an extraordinary enhancement.

7. TYPES OF DIGITIZATION

Many publishers are happy for you digitize the material yourself, provided it is an exact representation of the original published work and not modified in any way. Other publishers may request that you use their own digital copy of the work or obtain a copy from a trusted repository, digitized to a particular quality standard.

1. In-house Digitization

In-house digitization on the surface may appear to be an obvious solution, but you should consider carefully the staffing equipment costs of such a service. These will vary depending on the qualify of the files you are aiming to produce and the volume of material that you are hoping to purchase, but the minimum requirements for in-house digitization would be:

- Dedicated PC and scanner;
- Robust scanner, preferably with sheet feeder;
- Dedicated server space (with files typically 1 MB in

size, ensure the server has sufficient capacity for expansion); and
- Staff time to undertake scanning.

The purchase of the equipment may actually be the least of the problems associated with in-house digitization. One of the greatest challenges may be finding staff time to scan the material. The equipment also needs to be set-up ensure that material is scanned to an appropriate resolution that allows it to be read on screen or printed out, but does not result in excessively large files. Another important decision is whether to use optical character recognition (OCR) software to convert the material to text format. This will drastically reduce the file size, but does take additional time as documents need to be proofread to ensure errors have not been introduced and to remove artifacts such as line-break hyphens and page numbers.

2. Outsourced Digitization

Increasingly in the UK, institutions are looking to outsource digitization of core readings. This is particularly useful if staff and equipment are not available. In the UK the primary service offering digitization of such readings is the HERON service, which is not part of Ingenta UK. Outsourcing has several advantages, in particular:

- Staff time and equipment is not required to carry out the digitization work;
- Less staff training in new skills is necessary;
- The material does not have to be physically held by the library—such service generally acquire clean photocopies from the British Library; and
- Better qualities files are usually received—including text files, which are extremely, time consuming to produce in-house.

There are several disadvantages to using such a service, including:

- Material can take longer to process than in-house;

- The service is often less flexible than an in-house service;
- There may be higher overall costs; for example, the HERON Service typically;
- Charge approximately L30 per item for digitization, in addition to any;
- Copyright costs;
- If your collection has specialist material that cannot be obtained from the British Library it may be necessary to supply a digital copy or photocopy of *the article- so some* staff time is *still* associated with outsourced production; and
- There are obvious advantages to national or international *trust repositories* that can supply institutions with high-quality digitized materials. In the UK, the HERON Service is trying to build its reputation in this role. However, outside the UK, generally universities are continuing to scan articles individually as they are needed. However, with an increasing number of electronic journals and e-books, it is anticipated that demand for electronic reserves services may eventually reduce dramatically.

8. TRENDS IN DIGITIZATION

Libraries have gone through several generations of technology as they have evolved from print to electronic resources. Libraries are responding to the challenges of new technologies by taking the opportunity to redefine their fundamental role in the creation, distribution and provision of access to information.

Although information in electronic format was created with the advent of the computer in the 1950s, it was not until the early 1960s that the first database suitable for searching was developed. MEDLARS was the first on-demand computer-based information retrieval service, and it was developed primarily for the medical profession. In 1971, MEDLINE, the online version of MEDLARS, was the first major online dial-up database search service. In the following year, dialog offered the first public online commercial database. With these first databases, there were no real acquisition decisions, as they were offered as access services to which libraries could subscribe. Actual searching of these databases produced charges that many libraries passed along to users. While the information revolution was clearly underway, it was not until after the introduction of the CD-ROM in the mid-1980s that electronic resources began to have a major impact on selection practices in libraries.

Many of the first CD-ROM products offered to libraries were versions of larger online databases and were supplied on a subscription basis with ownership of the data remaining with the publisher/producer. Initially, the price of the product included licensing of the content and possibly the purchase of a computer and CD-ROM player as well. Products were guaranteed to work only with specified CD-ROM players, as standards were not yet established. The purchase of this equipment as part of the cost of the information product was not always easy. Often equipment was not considered an appropriate use of the library's materials budget. However, equipment budgets were not always large enough or flexible enough, initially, to accommodate this new demand. As with audiovisual materials, the unit price of these products was high and use was often limited to one individual at a time.

Although very expensive at first, CD-ROM products gradually became more affordable. As personal computers became widely available in most libraries, these products also became very popular. Initially, only one person could use these CD-ROM databases at a time, a major drawback, especially considering their high cost. The alternative was to purchase the needed database on magnetic tape and mount it or the local computer system, which could provide simultaneous access to many users. This, however, was a very expensive solution and one that most libraries could not afford. Gradually, hardware and software solutions were found that allowed several users to access the same CD-ROM database simultaneously. Some libraries even found ways to provide access to CD-ROM product to sites outside of the library.

As librarians grappled with these technological advances, they continued to make careful selection decisions for these high cost products. Most typically, a group that included subject specialists, reference librarians, instruction librarians, and technical staff made the selection decisions. However, just when librarians appeared to have mainstreamed the selection of electronic materials as they had audiovisual materials, another new technology arrived-the World Wide Web.

The World Wide Web permeates almost all aspects of computing. Ever-increasing arrays of information producers now rely on this media to distribute their products and services. The developments in electronic information, development of networked access and delivery of new library services has seen a radical transformation in the information chain.

The following are the distinct advantages of digitization:

- Information content can be retrieved remotely.
- Information content can be delivered directly to the end-user without human intervention.
- Digital content quality is extra ordinary and is improving on constant basis with the advancement in technology.
- Full text search facility is very powerful, sophisticated and hyper structural enabling cross collection resources for researchers.
- Digitization also enables a view system interface facility.
- Ways of delivery have improved not only in teaching but in learning and research process also.

9. ISSUES IN DIGITIZATION

Among the several issues in digitations, few issues grouped and the same is given below with their parameters.

- Legal Issues
    - o Copyright
    - o Contract
    - o Privacy
- Financial issues
    - o Financial Resources
    - o Changes to funding allocation

- Client issues
  - o Client needs
  - o Client attitudes
  - o Resistance to new technology
- Personal issues
  - o Staff Commitment to new system and service
  - o Changed staff training and competencies
  - o Professionalization
- Organization vs
  - o New organization structures
  - o Reorganization of Hierarchies and word driven
- Management issues
  - o Strategic planning
  - o Organizational support and leadership
  - o Appropriate statistical measurement
  - o Need for new or different performance measure
- Technological issues
  - o Security
  - o Infrastructure development
  - o Use of appropriate technology
  - o Standards
- Collaboration issues
  - o Resource sharing
  - o Co-operative purchasing of information resources
  - o Co-operative purchase or development of hardware and infrastructure
- Subject discipline issues
  - o Availability of content for different discipline to Appropriateness of delivery method

10. CONCLUSION

The digitization becomes a need of the day. Most of the documents are now available in the digital form. Further the preservation process towards longer duration makes the digitization becomes mandatory.

QUESTIONS

1. Write the different concept of Digitization.
2. What are the needs for Digitization.
3. Describe various Digitization Techniques.
4. Write the different types of Digitization.
5. Describe the various trends in Digitization.
6. Identify the various issues in Digitization.

16

Virtual Libraries

1. OBJECTIVES

1. Understanding the concept of Virtual Library
2. Describe the emergence of Virtual Library
3. Describe various characteristics of Virtual Library
4. Design and develop the Virtual Library

2. INTRODUCTION

Besides electronics books and journals, a virtual library can reference any kind of electronic material that has been published on the network. These materials include, for e.g. text documents, software, image, audio, databases, news groups, and other data repositories. An important part of the organization is that the items are the one which are relevant to the topic you wish to study so that there is not insurmountable extent of information to sift through as there would be if you accessed the Internet unaided. The purpose of a virtual library is to enable users to find relevant information, wherever it may reside on the Internet.

The virtual library exists independently of the amount or nature of the electronic information which it provides access to. There is no limit to the size, content or value of data in a virtual library. It's definition is shaped by individual or organizational need. Some early virtual libraries were simply sequential HTML files containing links to items on a particular topic and the files had to be manually searched for the relevant information. As the volume of relevant information explodes, this approach quickly becomes inadequate for all except the simplest topics.

3. EMERGENCE OF VIRTUAL LIBRARY

The virtual library formally opened its doors to the public in April, 1995 at Public Library of Chorlette and Mecklenburg County (PLCMC), North Carolina. According to Lois Kilkka, PLCMC new technologies manager, it was the demise of the library's collection of 16 mm films and phonograph records that led to the birth of the virtual library.

The PLCMC virtual library is a showcase for emerging communication technologies and electronic information access that serves as a community computer-learning laboratory.

The PLCMC captured the 1996 American Library Association/Information today, Inc "Library of the future" award for its virtual library—a. place where area residents can use and evaluate a multitude of software packages, multimedia CD-ROMs, and electronic information resources.

The PLCMC virtual library is a computer learning lab for the whole community. Visitors can travel the Internet, explore interactive multimedia, try out desktop publishing and imaging, and learn to use a variety of computer applications.

4. DEFINITIONS AND MEANING OF VIRTUAL LIBRARIES

The concept of "virtual libraries", is defined simplistically, embodies a phenomenon that any person who has a computer (or a terminal) and by which he can make a connection to the library network(s) can access not only the resources of that library but also access variety of information that is available nationally and internationally through networks, like the Internet, Intranet, without being physically present in the library. That is, virtual libraries provide its patrons the facility to use the information resources any time (some libraries may have time restrictions) and from virtually anywhere, provided the patrons have access to right :

(1) Multimedia capabilities that let the library users see graphics (eg. Maps in a geographic information systems) and listen to sound or voice; and
(2) Hypermedia capabilities that incorporate the techniques of hypertext and multimedia.

The virtual library according the Gretehen Reed "the information has to go where the people are, not *vice versa*. We have created an environment where essential information, expertise and data arc always available to every one one-day or night, at home or at work".

Timothy Green, Director of Business Research at the Centre for Business Knowledge (CBK) defines virtual library as "a *set* of services that gives customers the *knowledge they need to make the highest quality business decisions in the feast amount of time*".

Powell (1994), defined a virtual library as : "a library with little or no physical plant of books, periodicals, reading space or support staff but one that disseminates selective information directly to distributed library customers, usually electronically".

Gopen (1993) defines the virtual library as "Concept of remote access to networked world wide library and information sources. The library is as a synergy created by bringing together technologically the resources of many libraries and information services.

Thus, a Virtual library is a coherent, well-annotated indexed, and cross-referenced collection of Internet resources and the inter connecting pointers. A good virtual library has universal legibility of table of contents, indices, help files, good handling of all encoding system, completeness of coverage, good inter-resource navigation and differentiation between resources.

5. CHARACTERISTICS OF VIRTUAL LIBRARIES

Virtual libraries also called as Electronic libraries, online library or desktop library; in simple words it is electronic interaction of new library services with traditional library services.

The characteristics of **Virtual Library** are as follows:

- There is no corresponding physical collection,
- Documents will be available in electronic format,
- Documents are not stored in any location,
- Documents can be accessed from any workstation,
- Documents are retrieved and delivered as and when required, and
- Effective search and browse facilities are available.

6. DESIGNING AND DEVELOPING A VIRTUAL LIBRARY

1. Developing a Reference Framework of Technology Management

- By examining the structure and content of standard books, conference, classification/indexing systems, outline of teaching/training modules and scope of the programmes initiated by technology management centres.
- By refining the draft framework, which will be modified/adopted during the first three months and improved continuously thereafter.

2. Sourcing for Technology Management Information

- by identifying the key generators and users of technology including their policies and programmes,
- by browsing Internet using different search engines such as Yahoo, Altavista, etc.,
- by recording the URL address of relevant resources, on a standard pro-forma.

3. Evaluating and the Resources Used on a set of Relevant Parameters

- reputation and reliability of the originators,
- purpose of publishing,
- content and nature of presentation,
- relevance to technology management, and
- frequency and regularity of revision.

4. Annotating and Ranking URL Addresses

- annotating each URL addresses based on the content and presentation, and
- ranking the annotated URL address according to a point system based on reputation, reliability, purpose, presentations, relevance, frequency and regularity.

5. Organization of the URL Addresses

- classification of the addresses as per the reference framework,
- organization at similar URL address into modules/ segments,
- preparation of search aids or indexes wherever necessary,
- designing web pages for each module, and
- integrating the web pages with the help of the reference framework and providing suitable linkages.

6. Testing and Modification to the Virtual Library

- by demonstration to technology managers, and
- incorporating feedback received from the users.

7. Manual/Automatic Updating

- by monitoring new address announced in the web services and newsletters, and

- deploying a public domain software to automatically validate the virtual library linkages.

8. Monitoring and Performance Evaluation

- regular monitoring of the project, and
- analysing the performance on a half yearly basis and making course corrections if necessary.

7. CONCLUSION

A virtual library is not as vulnerable as its traditional counter part, because it is easier to "turn around a value added information package very quickly and cost effectively. In a virtual library things move very quickly and ensure that the vendors are able to keep up with. The university libraries are responding to the changing information milieu where desktop access to information resources is creating a networked environment. These will attempt to assist faculty/ researcher in the process of doing research within the confines of their own offices or computer laboratories. In a virtual library service, the information professionals require continuous learning and training so as to keep pace with vast array of resources and reaching to client expectations. But they are respected for their expertise. Therefore, the librarians/ Information professionals should establish virtual spaces where older physical collections can be used in new ways using new technologies. So far, there have been little efforts to construct virtual libraries in India. An exercise in this direction is essential to master the techniques and adopt it to our environment, and also to exploit the Internet access meaningfully.

QUESTIONS

1. What are the features of Virtual Libraries and state their functions?
2. State the advantages and limitations of Virtual Libraries.
3. Explain the characteristics of Virtual Libraries.

Bibliography

American Library Association, Task Force on Metadata, *Summary Report*. June 1999.

Adrienne Tannenbaum, Metadata Solutions: Using Metamodels, Repositories, XML, and Enterprise Portals to Generate Information on Demand, Addison-Wesley, 2002, ISBN 0-201-71976-2.

A.J. McGrail, E. Gulski, and *et. al*. "Data Mining Techniques to Asses the Condition of High Voltage Electrical Plant". *CIGRE WG 15.11 of Study Committee 15.*

Alessandro Valitutti, Carlo Strapparava, Oliviero Stock (2005). "Developing Affective Lexical Resources", *PsychNology Journal* (1): 61-83.

Andreas Doms, Michael Schroeder (2005). "GoPubMed: exploring PubMed with the Gene Ontology". *Nucleic Acids Research* 33: W783-W786. doi:10.1093/nar/gki470. PMID 15980585.

Summary: Daniel R. Masys (2001). "Linking microarray data to the literature". *Nature Genetics* 28: 9-10. doi:10.1038/ng0501-9 (inactive 2008-06-20).

Buyens, J. Step by step web data base Development, Microsoft Press P.H.I. New Delhi, 2000.

Bretherton, F.P. and Singley, P.T., 1994, Metadata: A User's View, Proceedings of the International Conference on Very Large Data Bases (VLDB), 1091-94.

Bo Pang, Lillian Lee, and Shivakumar Vaithyanathan (2002), "Thumbs up? Sentiment Classification using Machine Learning Techniques". *Proceedings* of the Conference on Empirical Methods in Natural Language Processing *(EMNLP)*: 79-86.

Berners-Lee, Tim; James Hendler and Ora Lassila (May 17, 2001). "The Semantic Web". *Scientific American Magazine.* Retrieved on 2008-03-26.

Berners-Lee, Tim; Fischetti, Mark (1999). Weaving the Web. HarperSanFrancisco, chapter 12. ISBN 9780062515872.

Berners-Lee, Tim (2001-05-01). "The Semantic Web". Scientific American. Retrieved on 2008-03-13.

Chip Pitts (March 15, 2007). "The End of Illegal Domestic Spying? Don't Count on It". *Wash. Spec...*

D.C.A. Bultermann, Is It Time For a Moratorium on Metadata?, *IEEE MultiMedia,* Oct.-Dec. 2004.

"Design Issues". W3C. Retrieved on 2008-03-13.

David Marco, Building and Managing the Meta Data Repository: A Full Lifecycle Guide, Wiley, 2000, ISBN 0-471-35523-2.

David, C. Hay, Data Model Patterns: A Metadata Map, Morgan Kaufman. 2006, ISBN 0-12-088798-3.

D. Hand, H. Mannila, P. Smyth (2001). *Principles of Data Mining*. MIT Press, Cambridge, MA. ISBN 0-262-08290-X.

Ellen Monk, Bret Wagner (2006). *Concepts in Enterprise Resource Planning, Second Edition*. Thomson Course Technology, Boston, MA. ISBN 0-619-21663-8.

Ellen Monk, Bret Wagner (2006). *Concepts in Enterprise Resource Planning, Second Edition*. Thomson Course Technology, Boston, M.A. ISBN 0-619-21663-8.

Guy, V. Tozer, Metadata Management for Information Control and Business Success, Artech House, 1999, ISBN 0-89006-280-3.

http://wwvv.odl.ox.ac.uk/metadata.htm

http://www.cs.cornell.edu/wya/DigLib/MS1999/Chapter4.html

http://web.engr.oregonstate.edu/~tgd/publications/kdd2000-dlft.pdf

Herman, Ivan (2008-03-12). "W3C Semantic Web Activity". W3C. Retrieved on 2008-03-13.

Herman, Ivan (2008-03-07). "Semantic Web Activity Statement". W3C. Retrieved on 2008-03-13.

http ://www.google.com

http : // www.ieee.org/ieeexplore

http : // www.msn.com

"IALEIA-LEIU Annual Conference in Boston on April 9, 2008".

1van Herman (2007). "State of the Semantic Web". *Semantic Days 2007*. Retrieved on 2007-07-26.

James Martin, Strategic Data Planning Methodologies, Prentice-Hall, Inc., Englewood Cliffs, New Jersey, 1982, p. 127

J.F. Superby, J.P. Vandamme, N. Meskens. "Determination of factors influencing the achievement of the first-year university students using data mining methods". *Workshop on Educational Data Mining, 2006.*

John Resig, Ankur Teredesai (2004). "A Framework for Mining Instant Messaging Services". *In Proceedings of the 2004 SIAMDM Conference.*

Kantardzic, Mehmed (2003). *Data Mining: Concepts, Models, Methods, and Algorithms*. John Wiley & Sons. ISBN 0471228524.

K.A. Taipale (December 15, 2003). "Data Mining and Domestic Security: Connecting the Dots to Make Sense of Data". *Colum. Sci. & Tech. L. Rev.* 5 (2). SSRN 546782/OCLC 45263753.

K. Bretonnel Cohen & Lawrence Hunter (January 2008). "Getting Started in Text Mining" ([dead ;omls] _ 2-9 & as_yhi = 2008 & btnG = Search Scholar search), PLoS *Computational Biology* 4(1): e20. doi:10.1371/ journal.pcbi.0040020.

Kristof Coussement, and Dirk Van den Poel (forthcoming 2008). "Integrating the Voice of Customers through Call Center Emails into a Decision Support System for Churn Prediction". *Information and Management.*

Liddell and Scott, *An Intermediate Greek-English Lexicon*, OUP, pp. 500ff.

Miller, M.A Data and Network Communications, Delmar Thomson Learning New Delhi, 2001.

Minoli, D. Internet and Intranet Engineering Technologies, Protocols and Applications, T.M.H., New Delhi, 1999.

Nigel Shadbolt, Wendy Hall, Tim Berners-Lee (2006). "The Semantic Web Revisited". *IEEE Intelligent Systems.* Retrieved on 2007-04-13.

Pandi, W.J. XML in Action Web Technology. P.H.I, New Delhi, 2001.

Ralph Kimball, *The Data Warehouse Lifecycle Toolkit,* Wiley, 1998, ISBN 0-471-25547-5

R. Todd Stephens (2003). Utilizing Metadata as a Knowledge Communication Tool. Proceedings of the International Professional Communication Conference 2004. Minneapolis, MN: Institute of Electrical and Electronics Engineers, Inc.

R. Baker, "Is Gaming the System State-or-Trait? Educational Data Mining Through the Multi-Contextual Application of a Validated Behavioral Model". *Workshop on Data Mining for User Modeling 2007.*

Stephen Haag *et. al. Management Information Systems for the information age,* p. 28. ISBN 0-07-095569-7.

Sklar, J. Principles of Web Design, Thomson Learning, New Delhi, 2001

Tor-Kristian Jenssen, Astrid Lsegreid, Jan Komorowskil & Eivind Hovig (2001). "A literature network of human genes for high-throughput analysis of gene expression". *Nature Genetics* 28: 21-28. doi:10.1038/ng0501-21 (inactive 2008-06-20).

Victoria Shannon (2006-06-26). "A 'more revolutionary' Web". *International Herald Tribune.* Retrieved on 2006-05-24.

William R. Durrell, *Data Administration: A Practical Guj^e to Data Administration,* McGraw-Hill, 1985.

W. Frawley and G. Piatetsky-Shapiro and C. Matheus (Fall 1992). "Knowledge Discovery in Databases: An Overview". Al Magazine: pp. 213-28. ISSN 0738-4602.

"W3C Semantic Web Frequently Asked Questions". W3C. Retrieved on 2008-03-13.

Xingquan Zhu, Ian Davidson (2007). *Knowledge Discovery and Data Mining: Challenges and Realities.* Hershey, New Your, p. 18. ISBN 978-159904252-7.

Yudong Chen, Yi Zhang, Jianming Hu, Xiang Li. "Traffic Data Analysis Using Kernel PCA and Self-Organizing Map". Intelligent Vehicles Symposium, 2006IEEE.

Index